LOVE TO THE MILLIONTH POWER

A Woman's Journey from Death to Love to Living in The Immortal Now

LOVE, SALVATION, AND SOUL MATES

The Story behind *Passage from Fear, Passage from Karma,* and *The Immortal Now*

PATRICIA GRABOW

AT ONE PRESS

At One Press
204 E. Callender St.
Livingston • MT • 59047
www.theimmortalnow.com

10 9 8 7 6 5 4 3 2 1

Printed in the United States of America

ISBN   978-0-9897146-0-0

Editor: Cheryl McLaughlin
Cover Designer: Laura Zugzda

This book is dedicated to my sons, Rob, Tim, and Chris. They are, by far, my greatest reason for being, and I have been blessed beyond measure by them. The book is also, with love and profound gratitude, dedicated to those whose stories grace these pages.

CONTENTS

SECTION ONE: *Passage from Fear*

Death in London, June 16, 1980 3
The Robe Well Woven 15
Now I See through a Glass Darkly 19
I Can Resist Everything—Possibly 25
In My Father's House Are Many Mansions 29
Pieces of the Puzzle Assemble Themselves 35
The Writing Begins 41
Other Lives, Other Loves 45
Messages Become Amazing 51
To the Oil Fields 57
Time to Go 63
Jackson, Wyoming 67
The New School 69
The Books Find a Setting 71
The Cayce Meeting 77
The Soul Mates 83
The Book Begins: *Passage from Fear* 87
Now, How Exactly Do You Do This? 95
The Books Become Easier 99
The Daily Schedule 105
The Wilson Stream 107
Skiing Down the Tetons 109
Endings, Beginnings, Forgiveness 111
Spring, Summer, and Baby 117
Robert Returns 123

SECTION TWO: *Passage from Karma*

The Second Book Begins: *Passage from Karma* 129
A World Changing 133
Alaska and Soul Mates 137
New Challenges 145
Another Life and the Source 149
We Finish Editing and Have Decisions to Make 161
I Return to Alaska 165
Leaving the North Slope 171

Filing EEOC Complaint 175
Robert Finds Me. 179
EEOC Complaint Hits the North Slope 181
The Search for an Attorney 185
The Lawsuit. 189
The Settlement 193

SECTION THREE: *Love to the Millionth Power*

I Raise My Children. 197
I Find Sister Works. 199
Firing and Irony 203
Publication of the First Book: *Passage from Fear*. 207
On to Fairbanks 215
Master's Degree 219
Off to Holy Cross and the Alaskan Bush. 221
We Almost Lose Robbie. 225
Town Looks Great 229
The Lower 48. 231
The Bed and Breakfast on Steroids. 233
We Republish *Passage from Fear* and Publish
    Passage from Karma. 237

SECTION FOUR: *The Immortal Now*

The Third Book, *The Immortal Now*,
    Comes into Being. 241
The Sessions Begin 247
Guidance Includes Charlotte and Arizona 251
The Guidance Sessions. 257

Epilogue. 263
Acknowledgments 269
Appendices
    White Light Meditation. 271
    Parts of Guidance Sessions 273

SECTION ONE

Passage from Fear

DEATH IN LONDON,
JUNE 16, 1980

Those who have had a near-death experience have understood this because, at that point, they visited their own Being. They visited the truth of the Truth and then emerged as individuals who understood that Larger Being.

-The Immortal Now

I never thought I would die in London.

Yet here I am, part of unlimited white light of pure, soft love to a millionth power—like being in love on a summer's day with the sun shining and feeling no separate reality. It is everything, and it is I. I have no words for it, only the indelible image of a child in a state of loving laughter being loosely covered over by a white satin blanket but without the identity of the child. It is like listening to music and being at the point where all that exists is the beauty of the symphony. The only experience in the entire universe is the joy of being enfolded by so much love. It has no periphery and no end. It is the white light of love, and I am bathed in an ocean of kindness without anything else. There is no separate self, no ego, no world, no struggle, no breath, nothing but the feelings I have ached for in a lifetime.

I am plunged into a soft, warm lake of all-encompassing compassion and joy and welcomed home. I am more alive than I had ever been, only it was not I.

The light is not a visual one but the light of love I have felt for a millisecond when my child smiled at me. That love to the millionth power permeates everything to the point where whatever I was on earth no longer exists and may never have existed. It is as if my heart exploded into the universe and is still within me—the unlimited part of me. It is love beyond any description, beyond any experience I have ever had within what we call life, soft beyond a down feather and broader than stars plunging into unlimited space. I am that love while experiencing it. It is I, and it is everything at once. There is no separate self.

Were I on the earth I would be sobbing, for it is all I ever wanted. It is what I sought in the love of my mate, the mountains, my children, the surf, the sun—anything that I loved with complete abandon. I am more alive now than I have ever been, only it was not I. It is not that I ceased to exist, but I am plunged into a soft, warm lake of all-encompassing compassion and joy and welcomed home. Everything and everyone is more alive, and everything is one—as love.

I am that love while experiencing it. It is I, and it is everything at once.

Then, the scene changed completely. I came "back" in an instant. I could feel my blood coursing through my veins and rushing into each capillary in my body. I could feel each hair strand sprouting from its follicle and smell the lumber in the walls with the scent of dead trees mixed with the odor of medicines and human sweat.

The incredible force of the entire earth's gravity pulled this body I had abandoned against the cold, metal table on which my body had been placed. With an overwhelming power I could not fight, it would not relinquish its hold. Sound was unbearable. I could hear my breathing and the rush of air to fill a physical body I was associated with, but not in. The unlimited love light remained within my heart space, but it was overwhelmed by this harsh and visual reality complete with a "me" in it—so different and apart from what I had just experienced. So outside. This must be what it feels like to be born—harsh, cold, and loud.

I looked up and caught the eyes of a woman in a blurred white dress looking sadly at me. She gasped. The woman yelled to others in the next room. A young man rushed in and began telling two other white blurs what needed to be done. Then there was a flurry of activity, and several people gathered around and began working on me.

I can still see that room today—linen white walls with a flat sienna ceiling and bricks somewhere. The walls were without names in my mind, only flat, blank spaces like a giant, hollow air-storage warehouse without any feeling. It was very cold.

As I looked out into the room, I realized that seeing was happening in my physical brain, and whatever I am was not yet a part of it. I saw figures—the nurse, the paramedic—moving in space as though I were somewhere else watching them. It was as if my senses had preceded the rest of me into the room. And I, the essence of me of which the physical was only a prism, was not quite ready to return. That part was still bathing and almost rolling in that unbelievable light of soft, unconditional, unlimited love. I think it always had been, and always would be, there.

A dark, young male in white and a blond attendant female appeared above me. The light above their heads almost gave them halos. Gently, the doctor said that I had a large tear from the edge of my eye, through my temple area and they were going to sew it up. They numbed the skin, and I could see the curved needle out of the corner of my eye as it rhythmically pierced and protruded from the flesh. When they finished, the male murmured something to the female and left my peripheral vision. She dutifully sat nearby keeping watch over me.

She seemed like an angel, in the membrane between life and death that was so thin for me. I know it was her job, but here she was in England, guarding someone from another country she did not know, as though she were a loving family member. She was, at that moment, a physical presence I could hold onto in my mind like an anchor to keep me with my children instead of returning to the white light that I wanted with all of my heart. I drifted off.

$\sim$

It had been a head-on collision in Kingston, a suburb of London, that brought on the whole experience. The paramedics from the Kingston Hospital pulled my limp body out of our rented Mini, a tiny British car, which had collided with a Mercedes Benz.

The accident happened in the late evening, in the rain, along busy British return-home-traffic side roads. I was on a frenetic trip, trying to show my two sons, fourteen and thirteen, that I could have fun even though my world at home in Alaska had just fallen apart one month earlier.

We were driving back from touring the Salisbury Cathedral and Stonehenge that day. I passed out from exhaust fumes in the car, I later concluded, and the Mini swerved into the other lane. We were headed for a gas station when we hit the Mercedes. My oldest son, Chris, was in the front seat. His left arm and leg broke on impact. Tim rode in the back and suffered only bruises.

$\sim$

Thank God for the British medical staff at the Kingston Hospital! They awakened me and brought my sons into the emergency room to see me. I was still in that intermediate stage between worlds, immobile like a paralyzed witness. Seeing with my eyes was still a conscious decision.

The staff wheeled Tim in first. I had to turn my eyes to see him without moving my head. I could catch him slightly. He burst out of the wheelchair, and when our eyes met, he stood for a moment to be sure that what they had said was true. Beaming, he sat back in the chair with the nurse behind him.

At the same time, nurses pushed Chris in on a metal gurney and pulled it adjacent to my table. "Mom!" he murmured as he tried to get up for a hug and then fell back, overwhelmed by the pain of his own injuries.

The moment I saw the sons I loved so very much, the rest of me flooded back into the room. All of us were enveloped in that light, and I felt a kind of peacefulness in chaos that everything on some level was right.

The medical staff took my sons to the adjacent rooms. I could feel them leaving and desperately wanted to get up and care for them, but I could not move. I was their mother who needed to tend to their wounds and was not accepting that I, too, was wounded.

After they left, it felt as if the light of love to the millionth power I had experienced when I died was behind a dark fabric poked with tiny holes. Life, here, was that fabric where the love streamed through the holes for just a millisecond, showing up in experiences like watching my children when they were sleeping or rolling in the snow or smelling a flower or laughing at a completely silly joke.

I had seen the beauty of that light as it found its way through the patchwork of green leaves in a Douglas fir forest on the Washington coast, and in crystalline waters of a high mountain lake where the light shimmered on the bottom rocks making them look as if they were water. That love had always been present. I was suddenly aware of it all and could hardly breathe, sobbing inside with a painful joy. With every fiber of my being, I wanted to be completely lost in it again, but I had to be back where those I loved needed me.

Whatever I am as a being, not dependent on the existence of a body, came back from my death in London and found itself in great physical and emotional pain. Because my father died when I was ten years old, I did not want my children to miss me as I had missed him for a lifetime.

Looking back, I realized I had experienced several stages to existence: one where the individual is entirely of the physical world—what we call "living"; second, a transitional stage where the individual as a loving spirit can experience this plane of existence intellectually but does not need to be present physically; and third, what some might call death but isn't. It is life with the white light of love. The individual is part of all life in the present time, in The Immortal Now.

So, what if what we call death is simply being present with the Presence of all things in absolute love? What if the state of being I experienced when I died was simply who I am, one with everything, all of the time? What if there really is no time? What if there is no sequence of life, death, heaven? What if all experience is simply love in the present?

What if what we call death is simply not death at all, but life?

Lying helpless on a gurney with a broken body, I realized that all that had ever existed was that love to the millionth power I had just experienced. It is like a fish becoming aware, in awe, that it lives in water! I was filled and flowing with the love in which I was engulfed. What if what we call death is simply not death at all, but life? What if what we have called reality is more like an image on a mirror?

At the time, I was struggling to move to that mirror—to be physically present—because of the love in my heart for my sons. It took everything I had to do so. I faded off again.

I awoke in a small, Spartan room with high ceilings and bricks I could see out the windows. I must be on a higher floor, I thought, or I would be seeing trees. The bed was a black, narrow single cot with white linens and a nightstand to my left. It must have been late afternoon since the light was beginning to dim. I drifted in and out of consciousness.

Unbeknownst to me, my sons' father and my ex-husband, Walter, flew in from Paris the next day. He was a TV evening news correspondent at the time, and the network let him come to London as soon as he found out about the accident. We had married fourteen years earlier, but during the last eight years after our divorce, I had hardly seen him. Chris and our second son, Tim, had maintained contact.

Out of the blue, Walter walked into the room and looked down at me with his dark eyebrows twisted with concern.

"If it hadn't been for your mother, Pat, our marriage would have lasted," he said.

The non-sequitur nature of what he said surprised me, and I didn't have any idea of how to respond. True, my mother and Walt had never gotten along during what was for me, a stifling six-year marriage, but at the moment I was desperate for information about what had happened to our children. I asked him if he had seen the boys.

"They have Chris upstairs. He has a broken femur and right arm. He is going to have to stay in traction on his back for a full month. Patty, what the hell happened?"

I could not stand it. I cried out loud. The grief for my optimistic, joyous son overwhelmed me.

Walter paused.

"Chris will be okay," he said. "He just asks about you. Tim is a different story. They have discharged him, but with you and Chris in the hospital, I really don't know what to do with him. I had to set him up in a bed and breakfast next to the hospital. The people are very nice but distrustful of Americans. They assured me that they will take good care of him. The hospital had to discharge him, you know. He really wasn't hurt, so they couldn't just keep him here."

I didn't know. No one had told me.

"He's going to be okay there. He can come see you as often as he likes."

I learned later, that Tim was not allowed to visit me.

"I can stay only a day more," Walter said in his matter-of-fact way. "The network needs me, and you know how it is. I have to get back to Paris."

His highly competitive job had become his demanding passion. The network dictated the terms of his life, and he had to do whatever they wanted as they could always find an ambitious young journalist to replace him. I knew what the pressure was like. I had experienced it vicariously for the duration of our marriage.

We visited briefly, and then he left. I watched him as he turned and said good-bye. Physically, he had not changed. He was two inches shorter than I, with wide shoulders, long arms, and dark, expressive eyes. As he spoke, it had always charmed me that the corners of his mouth turned down no matter what he said. He was quick to laugh but with humor that could be biting. I was grateful he had come for the boys' sake, but so often I felt discomfort in his presence, especially now when I was defenseless.

The next few days passed within the protocol of the British socialized medical system. I would lie in my little bed, interrupted only by the nurses' care and the irregular and unannounced visits by a neatly dressed doctor in a frock coat with an entourage of three or four interns.

They would walk in together. The doctor would stand at the end of the bed and explain something to those who had surrounded me on either side. They never looked at me but kept their eyes on the doctor the entire time unless he specifically directed them to look at a particular part of my anatomy. He would say something, and then they would murmur respectfully in reply. He, always a he, would move to the side of the bed, examine me, say something to those around him, and then the entire party would leave.

I tried to talk to them. "Excuse me, doctor, but what were my injuries in the accident?"

The doctor would let out a nervous, "Harrumph," and look away. No one in the entourage would speak.

"Hello, if you would not mind too much, could you tell me what happened during that accident I was in? I don't remember it too well."

No response.

"If you could, could you at least tell me how long I will be hospitalized?" I was beginning to feel like a character in a Peter Sellers movie.

There was uncomfortable movement in the entourage, and then they walked to the door and on out.

"Please, come back. I have just a couple more questions … Okay, you can come back now—I said you can come back now."

In a quiet frenzy, I rang for the nurse. She came in quickly.

"Yes, what can I do for you?"

By then, the doctor had handed off information regarding my care to her, and she repeated what he said, which was very little. At no point in my short stay at the hospital was I told by a doctor anything regarding what was going on, not that I didn't try to ask again the next time they came in to examine me.

I found out a few pieces of information from the nurse but lacked a direct explanation. At first, they thought my neck was broken, but it was not so. It was damaged. I had broken several ribs, separated my clavicle from my sternum, and had suffered severe lacerations to my head, including the temple.

The rest of the time, I lay in my bed worrying about my children and trying not to think about the events that had led up to the accident. Then the florist delivered roses from Robert—the man who had just torn apart my world one month earlier.

I stared at the note that said something to the effect that he was sorry about the accident and that was all he had to say. I stared at the flowers. He was sorry about the accident and wanted me to be sure that was all? He found out about the accident and sent a small bouquet of flowers? I could not believe it.

This was the man who told me only a month earlier, when we had been in love for a year-and-a-half—I had thought: "This whole relationship was for revenge. I wanted you in a position where you lost everything, and you have: your house, your husband, and your children. I've done what I wanted. I'm leaving now. I never divorced my wife and have bought her a house in Idaho, and I'm going to work for the oil company on the North Slope. Good-bye, Pat."

Then he walked out of the door.

I lost my speaking voice right there for three days and had spent the last month trying to put the pieces of myself back together—and now the accident, and then the flowers, reminding me of Robert.

I reached bottom.

I had no illusions, no courage, and no escape left. I could no longer seek optimism as a source of strength. I faced a chasm of fear and sorrow so great that the ends of my fingers tingled and hurt. Breath came hard.

THE ROBE WELL WOVEN

When we recall loving someone completely, that moment is
forever. It is not that that is ever dissolved. It is never dissolved.
It does not dissolve, as the individual never dissolves.

-*The Immortal Now*

I could hardly remember what my life was like before Robert pierced it like a dagger.

The best word for my "before Robert" state was contentment but not quite complacency. I was carving a life out of the things I loved most. My second husband, David, and I had been through some rough times in our six-year marriage and had decided to make a go of it. We had just finished building a beautiful log house in a naturally wooded piece of land twenty-five miles north of Anchorage, Alaska. The property sloped down sharply to a rushing stream, called Peter's Creek, in the small rural community of Chugiak. The windows of the log house looked out through an eight-foot porch onto the regal Chugach Mountains. David and I had carefully planned the placement of the house so the view could be a part of our daily lives. In the course of the day, I would wander almost subconsciously to where the view was best and check the moods of the mountains.

The Chugach Mountains had so many dimensions—physical and spiritual. Sometimes they would shroud themselves in thin veils. Sometimes they would stand bright as teenage girls getting their pictures taken. Sometimes they would show off the frosting of newly fallen snow, but they always appeared mysterious and created for me the emotion of beauty. Beauty is a feeling that I did not understand or appreciate until I lost it. I had known David since we were college sweethearts my freshman year. During my junior year, I left school to marry Walter. Three months after I left Walter, David and I met up again. Since David's greatest love was the land and I had grown up in Montana and always loved the out-of-doors, we courted by climbing mountains, canoeing streams, and hiking beaches. After we were married, we went back to school at the University of Washington. David worked on completing his master's degree in biology, beginning the first study of the North American Black Oystercatcher, a coastal seabird. I earned my BA and teacher's certificate. We lived with the boys on a thirty-six-foot sailboat for a couple of years—an Adkins hull sloop called *The Spray*—with the excuse of studying seabirds. Then we chose to go to Chugiak, Alaska. David was going to work for the US Fish and Wildlife offices. I was applying for teaching jobs.

I had read the *Foxfire* books by Elliot Wiggington, which were based on an experimental high school educational program where students from rural Appalachian communities helped preserve local traditions of their culture. They captured oral histories, created how to do it articles to pass on cultural skills and traditions, such as how to weave Appalachian baskets, gathered other material for publication in a book. My dream was to do a similar program among Alaska Native students. When David and I moved to Anchorage, I opened a newspaper, and what did I see but an ad for a teacher for a Foxfire-type program with Alaska Native students in Bethel, a remote hub for rural Alaska! I took the job, left my husband working in Chugiak, and boarded in Bethel for six months.

I taught high school Yup'ik Eskimo students English and flew ninety-six students to the small, remote, traditional villages, scattered across western Alaska, from which they had come. The students collected legends, stories, and how-to-do-it articles. When the students returned to Bethel Regional High School, as it was called, they translated their stories from Yup'ik to English and laid out their stories for publication. We published it in a book titled, *Kalikaq Yugnek*, "the book that comes up from the people."

After the job in Bethel, I returned to David in Chugiak and found a job with the Indian Education program working with the traditional Native people I loved through the Anchorage School District. I was living the script I had written, doing what I wanted, and acting out my fantasy and the fulfillment of my dreams.

My children played starring roles in it, as well. I had custody of my two sons, Chris and Tim, and I adored them. I would sometimes walk the kids to the excellent new elementary school down a birch-and-conifer-tree-lined road and up the knoll. The kids had their favorite sights as they walked—the cat they liked, the trash can at the furniture store where Chris found furnishings for his tree house, or the friends that would join in on the early morning school trek.

So there, I had it all. I had my husband, my work, my children, and at last, the home of my choice. Suffice it to say, it never occurred to me that I would not be married to David forever in spite of whatever challenge came along. David was my husband but more like the friend who stood by me for whatever reason, like the seasons, varied yet always there, and had been so for almost seven years.

What could go wrong? The unraveling of the robe well woven is not an easy task.

Now I See through a Glass Darkly

You will see that the truth is passion in everything. It is simple, a simple love. It is a simple power. It is primarily in the seeking, in the perceiving, in the heart that chooses not to stop life as a process.

–The Immortal Now

It began with a completely unexpected phone call. In retrospect, I am not sure that we do not choose our pain and, perhaps, our individual path to redemption, as well as our contentment.

It was dusk, and the light was filtering through the windows of our home in Chugiak, giving the logs a golden hue. The boys, then eleven and twelve, were upstairs, doing their homework. David was doing finishing work on the wall of the living room.

"Pat, there is a phone call for you," David called out.

"Who is it?" I asked.

"Some man who said that you might not remember him. Interesting, huh."

"Fine, give me the phone. … Hello, this is Pat."

A voice I did not recognize came from the other end of the line.

"I called your mother, and she said you were in Anchorage. I couldn't believe it. This is Bob. There is no way you are going to be in Anchorage without me seeing you."

I know that I was silent too long, trying to remember who Bob was.

"You don't remember me, do you?"

"I'm sorry. I don't," I said.

"Do you remember hitchhiking with me in Yellowstone and then my coming through the University of Washington? I worked in the kitchen when you were waitressing at Old Faithful Inn. The tall one. The one who asked you to marry him sixteen years ago."

Then it hit me. Yes, I had waitressed at Old Faithful Inn when I was eighteen years old, and there was a seventeen-year-old who was six-feet-ten-inches tall, working in the kitchen. He was thin, dark, with heavy eyebrows, and I remember thinking uncharitably that he looked like a tree with ears.

Robert was like a pesky puppy dog who always needed my attention. At the time, I was obsessed with my first love, Tony from Montana, and had no interest in Robert except as a hitch-hiking partner. I needed someone to pair up with while I used my thumb for transportation to my mountain-climbing class in Jackson Hole, Wyoming, and he was more than willing to come with me.

At the time, I wondered why we didn't get rides but later realized that few people were willing to pick up a six-foot-ten-inch man and a six-foot-tall woman, no matter how desperate they looked. Consequently, Robert and I spent chunks of our time by the side of the road, visiting about the meaning of life and batting an occasional mosquito. Finally, someone would stop and stuff us on top of the camping gear in the back of the station wagon or sit us in the back of the pick-up truck.

Robert was surprisingly bright and insightful during our talks—slightly cynical, but he could stay on track in a debate. One time, I took the Grand Inquisitor scene from Dostoyevsky's *Brothers Karamazov*, arguing that everything was basically good by degrees and that there was no evil. He did not exactly refute it but deftly skirted around it, questioning my premise.

Two years after that summer, while I was a student at the University of Washington, I received a similar call from Bob. Out-of-the-blue phone calls must have been his forte.

"This is Robert. I have a ring in my pocket, and I'm on my way to Alaska. Will you marry me?"

Just like that—will you marry me?

He said later that I had laughed, but I had not. I could not, for the life of me, remember who he was. There had been a long pause.

He interjected something at that time about Old Faithful Inn and his being tall and that he had rescued me when I needed a hitchhiking partner. I began to remember who he was.

"Oh, yes—"

"Will you marry me?" he interrupted.

I had not known what to say and remember asking him if he could come over to McKee Hall, the dormitory I was living in, and talk about it.

"No, I can't. My plane will be taking off in an hour," he had said. "I have a one-way ticket and twelve dollars in my pocket. I couldn't even pay for a cab to your dorm." He then mumbled something about having to leave and hung up.

I remember shaking my head in disbelief the rest of that day, thinking about the phone call and mumbling something about it not being real. It was a dream, and like a sliver in a hand, it really was not part of me, but I could not remove it easily.

Now, sixteen years later, it was déjà vu.

"Yes, Robert, now I remember you," I responded.

"So when can I see you?"

"I'm married, Robert," I replied.

"Bob," he said matter-of-factly.

"Okay, Bob."

"Yeah, your mother told me about David. I have the name right, don't I?"

"Yes."

"Yeah. I'm married, too. So what? When can I see you?"

"I don't think you understand what I am saying, Bob. It might not be a good idea."

"I think I said that there is no way that we are both going to be in Anchorage without my seeing you."

"Well, if we meet as friends, then, maybe okay," I said hesitantly. "I didn't mean to be rude, you know. You had to put forth a lot of effort in finding my phone number. I'm sorry."

"Good. You know the Log Cabin Bar on Muldoon near the Glenn Highway? I'll meet you there at six o'clock tomorrow night. Good-bye."

And that was it—no visiting about what had been going on for the last sixteen years, no discussion of children, family, home. I guess he had found out what he wanted from his conversation with my mother. I just didn't know what to think. He was being so rude and inconsiderate of his wife. I could simply ignore the call and not show up. But I had said I would. I told David about the call and drove to the Log Cabin Bar the next day.

The bar was dark with a log extension to the right of the entryway. Small round tables to the left of the door cozied around the small dance floor. I looked around and saw no one as tall as Bob and decided to sit at one of the round tables. I was relieved and thought that if he did not show up, I would leave. Then, when he would call again, I would have my excuse. I would say that I could not see him, and that would be that. End of story.

As soon as I resolved this in my mind, a tall, full-figured man, dressed in a gray, three-piece business suit got up, drink in hand, and began walking toward me. I remember thinking this must be Bob, but he did not look anything like the person I vaguely remembered. He stopped at my table and sat down next to me.

"Pat?"

"Yes, I'm Pat." I guess I didn't look the same either.

"I'm Bob."

"Bob. I'm sorry, I really didn't recognize you." There I was, apologizing again. "You really have changed."

"So have you," he replied. "You're heavier."

"Really? I hadn't noticed." Was that ever a lie!

Robert, I learned, used carefully chosen, often biting, words to create an effect with just enough truth to catch people off-guard but not leave them entirely speechless. You just say dumb things.

We talked for a while the way adults are supposed to. We discussed our relationships, children, jobs—just the normal conversation between two people who were married to other people—courteous, polite, and distant. Just right.

He had a wife, whom he referred to as his "mouse wife," and two young children. When he first arrived in Anchorage, he worked as a bouncer at the Montana Bar on Fourth Avenue. Then he went to law school because he said I told him that someday I was going to go to law school and he did not want me to best him. He now worked for a company that built the multimillion-dollar gathering stations on the North Slope oil fields during the Alaska pipeline and had become a vice-president of sorts.

Then, out of the blue, he leaned his massive body across the distance between us, placed his hand at the back of my neck, pulled me to him, and kissed me. He held on through my initial shock until I found myself responding to him. I was more surprised at myself than him when he finally let go and was just catching my breath when he got up from the table.

"You *will* see me again," he said as he turned and left.

I drove the entire twenty-five miles back to Chugiak, engaged in a dialogue with an imaginary Bob sitting next to me:

"Dream on, Bob. I will *not* see you again, Bob. Not on your friggin' life, buddy!"

Eventually, I did.

I CAN RESIST
EVERYTHING—POSSIBLY

You will see that the life that you have created for yourself is
that of the dreamer in the dream.

–*The Immortal Now*

All of my life, I was one of those students who loved school and chose to excel academically. I was also the most ecumenical spiritual seeker I knew in high school, considering the fact that I lived in small towns. During my sophomore year in high school in Libby, Montana, I alternated between attending the Christian Science Sunday school and singing in the Presbyterian choir on Sunday mornings. After school, I would go to the Catholic Youth Organization with my friend, and I was also the president of the Methodist Youth Organization. I had an enormous appetite for reading everything about Buddhism, the Tao, western philosophers, and the Gita and loved that thread of guidance for human behavior in whatever religious traditions I encountered. As an undergraduate, I majored in English. I truly wanted to know what this life was all about and believed that if I read enough, someone out there might explain everything through that medium which I loved most: the written word.

So, how did I ever get caught up in Robert's world?

Robert began to call me daily at work. At the time, I was in charge of the Native tutors for the Anchorage School District through the Indian Education program. I tried to be polite to Robert, but finally I told the secretary not to forward any of his calls. Robert then took a different tack and started showing up at my office as I was getting off work. To make a long story short, I finally met up with him, and that is when the story Robert spun for the two of us began its life within my heart.

Robert kept telling me that he had always been in love with me, that he was in love with me now, and that he wanted us to have a life together. I was the reason he was born, he said, and he knew it the moment he saw me in Yellowstone. To feel so wanted in someone's life was something I wanted to hear. While my relationship with David had been getting better, he was more of an intellectual and distant emotionally. Robert was intellectual and passionate. Only later did I discover that Robert was like a chameleon who would tell you what you wanted to hear and behave like the person he knew you wanted him to be.

We began an affair. I was fraught with guilt, but Robert assured me that things would work out. He told me he was going to leave his wife, but first he had to make sure she was financially secure since they had two children.

He told me how much he wanted us to have children, which never happened during my marriage to David. Robert wrote love letters to me asking me to remove my birth control, flew my mother up for Christmas, and said he would do anything to have me understand how much he loved and wanted me. We flew to San Diego, ate Chateaubriand at the Hotel del Coronado, flew to Los Angeles in the evening for drinks at the Playboy Club, and watched a performance of *Annie*. On the way back, we stopped off in San Francisco and stayed at the St. Francis Hotel, all on his company nickel.

Somewhere in the mix, I fell in love with him.

I foolishly assumed that what Robert told me was true. Raised in Montana as a truth-sayer by a western family, much like those in the Midwest, I believed in a moral code of conduct and assumed that was true of others. Now I was left with a choice of my own. Would I continue my marriage to David, or would I make the commitment to Robert?

By my ethical standards, I could not continue with David were I to be involved with Robert so I decided, and then asked, David for a divorce. Simple as that. I left everything I had dreamed of with the wave of the wand of decision, of commitment to Robert, and assumed that he had done the same. One can call it the mistake of my life, which it was, and one can call it fated so that everything that followed could happen. I think both are true.

In My Father's House Are Many Mansions

Empathy is understanding the nature of oneness. Empathy exists within the heart. Empathy does not exist within the head.

–*The Immortal Now*

Five days after the accident, I was ambulatory and desperate with worry about Tim in the bed and breakfast. I was discharged from the hospital and moved into the room Walter had found for him. Walt was right. The room was very close to the hospital. As you left the emergency room and crossed twenty feet of lawn, there was a red brick, two-story house that served as a bed and breakfast. Our room was at the top of a narrow hallway as you came into the building. Tim helped me up the steps.

The owner and his daughter had their living quarters in a small area on the first floor. Both were extremely wary of Americans. I seldom saw them except when it was time to pay the room rent, which they insisted on ahead of time. With my injuries, I could not blame them for shying away and being focused on the money.

Tim was very happy to have Mom back. He and I took my things to the room and immediately went back to the hospital to see Chris. It was almost like picking up the pieces of shattered glass from the accident—first Tim, then Chris.

I asked Chris about what had happened to him in the hospital.

"Oh, it wasn't so bad, Mom."

But I knew that a broken femur was one of the most painful experiences a person can have.

Chris was a master of masking the pain. "Not so bad" compared to what?

"Mom, I'm okay."

"What did they tell you?"

"The nurse said that I have to stay here for a month, like Dad said. They put pins in my leg. Dad says that he'll send books for me to read."

My heart ached beyond tolerance. Every minute ripped me apart, leaving a gaping hollow space that nothing could fill. How could Chris have so much hope when mine was gone? I loved my sons completely, but for the first time in my life, I was like the living dead. I presented the body they loved as Mom, but something inside was different from the mother they knew—someone lost in grief along with an inarticulate spiritual longing that occupied every cell of my body.

Part of me was in total empathy with my beloved Chris's pain. It was as though there were no words to convey our feelings so we were reduced to a primitive form of sign language or the genetic remembrance of mother and son. Maybe the mother/son relationship was enough, but I struggled to surface with words in some form to say what must be said to encourage this courageous young son of mine. He was bearing the aftermath of the holocaust we had all just been through and was doing his best just to stay positive, survive, and move on. He had no words or energy for anything else. It was as though a sleeping bear was in the room when we communicated, even by phone. Were we to say anything that was not optimistic, the bear would awaken and devour us. We were constantly afraid of that bear.

I could not take any of Chris's agony away from him, no matter how hard every instinct in my body ached to stand between him and what he was facing. I could not pull myself back from the living dead. I was like a mother bear flailing at the wind, trying to feign off a phantom attacker knowing there was nothing she could do to help her young. I could be there physically, but he had to survive with his own will to live.

The days passed in slow motion.

Walter had a friend in London, John, who made arrangements for a relative of his to take Tim and me into their home. It was during the Wimbledon tennis tournament, which was close to their pleasant, two-story brick house. The whole family was like a British version of *Life with Father*. The children bounced in and out of their house in their merry pursuit of life in England's middle-class world. John decided, at my request, to take me to a solicitor, the British term for an attorney, regarding the Mini and the exhaust fumes that had caused the accident.

I was still recuperating from my injuries when we met with the British solicitor. John told me that he would say everything—that it would not be appropriate for me, as a woman, to tell my story directly to the solicitor. That was the British way. Being the offspring of Montana pioneer women (one of whom traversed half of the United States in an ox-drawn covered wagon and bore and raised nine children in anything but civilization), not speaking was completely alien to me.

I tried my best to talk to John and let him speak to the solicitor. Knowing that we were speaking the same language, basic English, which we had all learned as our mother tongue, it seemed odd not to talk directly to the man in a brown suit sitting across from me behind the large, polished desk he earned from attending law school. Obediently, I told John what happened, and John would then tell the solicitor. The two men appeared to think nothing about the parts we were all playing.

I kept trying to suppress my chuckles when John didn't quite get what I was saying and the solicitor would politely correct him, for he understood everything I had just said. The net result of the meeting was that it would be unreasonable for me, as an American and a woman in the situation I was in, to sue the "car hire" company. So much for that. They talked; they agreed. It was their country and their legal system. They made my decision for me. But, at the time, I was without choice.

John and Walter then had a conversation and decided that Tim would go back to Washington, D.C., to stay with his father. When I recovered enough to travel, they told me arrangements had been made for me to go back to the United States and stay with my sister. They concluded, after speaking with the solicitor, that it was best for me to leave the country due to the cost, my need for help during my recovery, the lack of support in England, and the concern that the car hire company might sue me. Although I knew them to be at fault, the car hire company put the onus on me to prove that exhaust fumes had caused the accident and the damage to the vehicle rather than, as they would maintain, negligent driving. It meant, however, leaving my beloved son behind for the remaining month he was to be in the hospital under the care, gratefully, of British socialized medicine. Walter and John promised that Chris would have daily visits.

Two weeks after the accident, I boarded a 747 to Seattle with the plan to go on to Moscow, Idaho, to my sister Gretchen's home. It was as though somewhere I had fallen into rushing water and went along with where the stream carried me. I had no paddle and watched my son stay on the shore as I disappeared helplessly down the river.

The aching guilt of leaving Chris behind in the hospital, coupled with the events that led up to the accident, were overwhelming, but still not enough to account for the complete depression I was experiencing. I simply did not want to be here on the earth as a human being but knew I had to be. What I wanted was the love I had felt when I had died. Being here as a person was intolerably painful, and there was nothing I could do to fight it, overcome it, or get around it.

PIECES OF THE PUZZLE
ASSEMBLE THEMSELVES

*You are truly moving beyond the need for death. Death is
only a creation. It is only part of a belief system. What exists
does not die, and one does not need the vehicle of death in
order to connect with what exists. It is truly a belief.
It is truly a projection upon the mirror.
It does not relate to the nature of reality.*

−The Immortal Now

Gretchen, my sister, picked me up at SeaTac and was horri-
fied at what she saw—her sister still injured, arm in a sling,
and depressed beyond anything she had ever seen. She tried
everything she knew to cheer me up, but nothing could be done.
I was in a daze and could not believe that I had left London.

"Patty," Gretchen said, "Kip and I have planned a bicycle
trip to the San Juan Islands."

Was I hearing right? A bicycle trip? A bicycle trip! I
thought I was coming back to heal from my injuries and
figure out how to get back to Chris. The physical pain alone
made me feel as if I was encased in cement. I could not move.
The emotional pain I could not describe was one hundred
times greater. I could not sleep. I could not stay awake. I just
wanted to sleep to forget what was going on, and Gretchen
and Kip planned a bicycle trip?

The San Juan Islands in Washington are one of the most
beautiful places in the United States to me—blue lulling ocean,
pine-covered islands sleepily absorbing the rolling of the waves,
and white and green ferries connecting them, looking almost

like children's toys as they approached from a distance. I loved everything about the islands and had dreamed of living there. Gretchen and Kip told me that they would not be going home to Idaho until after the trip and they really did not want me to go to there alone. I agreed to go to the San Juans, but the disconnect was stark, and I could not hide my pain. I would have to go slowly with my injuries, and I could not put up things like tents.

We bicycled and camped for four days, and I could hardly breathe without crying, much less be my old self. There was no old self. The love I felt during my death was still in my heart like a brilliant light that illuminated everything inside. It felt like a white hole pulling me into it with a force stronger than I could resist. I was a shell of a being, looking out from its eyes, and joy, peace, and love were not in the body I was hauling around.

When Gretchen and Kip were not looking, I would disappear into the woods and sob uncontrollably. I called Chris whenever I could get to a phone. England was so far away. Finally, after cycling around Orcas, Lopez, and other islands, we returned by ferry to Anacortes and the mainland.

I turned to Gretchen after picking up my car, "You and Kip go on to Moscow. I'll make it over in a couple of days."

"Don't stay here, Patty. Please. You need to be with others now."

"No, really. I'll be all right. There are just some things I need to take care of."

"Like what, specifically?"

"Nothing, really. I just desperately need to be alone right now."

"Patty, you don't. I am so worried about you—I'm almost as desperate as you are. Patty, if you want to know the truth, I've never seen you like this. I'm actually afraid for your life."

"Gretchen, what makes you say that?"

"I just know. Promise me you won't attempt suicide. I know that sounds far out, but I don't know how to say it any other way. I mean just that. Promise me. That is the only way I will leave you here."

"I promise," I said.

She was not reassured, but I promised enough so she finally gave in. She knew I never broke my word—until now when it could be irreparable. Gretchen said later that she never prayed so hard in her life as that night when she left me at Anacortes and drove the 350 miles to her home in Idaho.

I found a cheap motel right away.

I had never harbored the fantasy of suicide, but that night, my sister knew exactly what I was thinking. I was in an emotional pain as severe as the broken femur my son had suffered, and there was no relief anywhere. I could see no other way out. Not even my love for my children was enough to stop me now. Nothing was. I would lie to my sister, do anything to stop the pain—anything. Robert was right. I had lost everything. I didn't care about anything. I really did not want to take my life. I just wanted the pain to go away and find just a millisecond of peace.

Pierre Teilhard de Chardin, a nineteenth-century monk and philosopher, once wrote, "Joy is the most infallible sign of the presence of God." I had no joy. I was starkly alone, doubled over in gut-wrenching pain I had never known before, lost in a crumbling illusion like an image on a mirror of shattered glass. I was without the presence of God in any corner of my life.

I remembered, at one point in my relationship with Robert, we were talking about life in general. He asked me, "If you could have anything, what would you want?"

"You really mean that? If I could have anything at all?"

"Anything."

"The truth is that what I want will sound funny to you."

"I'll try to contain myself," he said.

"Well, you know the phrase from the Bible, 'Now we see through a glass, darkly, but then face to face'? I never again want to see through that glass darkly. I want to know. I don't want to guess that a given philosophy or credo is the truth. I want to know what the truth is with certainty. I want to know who this 'I' is and what I am doing here. I want to know why it all is the way it is. I mean it, Robert. If I could have one wish, truthfully, that would be it. In a sense, I would see God face to face."

I then asked him what he would have, if he could have anything. His answer shocked me.

"Have you ever wanted to commit the perfect crime?"

Now, ironically, there I was in my motel room, without Robert and with my wish granted. I had my moment when I died, when I did not "see through a glass, darkly." I saw love beyond anything I had ever imagined face to face. Who would have ever thought that, once my prayer was answered, my only thought would be to end my life?

That night was endless. I was Jacob wrestling. I was every archetype I knew of those who had lived before me in every tragedy written, who had struggled and writhed, attempting to circumvent the ancient will to live with the need to end the pain. In the middle of the night, I called a Christian Science practitioner that David and I had met when he had been at Fort Lewis and asked him to pray for me as I was unable to reach out to anything—anywhere. At dawn, I found I had survived the night.

I drove to Moscow, Idaho, the next day, but the struggle was obvious to my sister and Kip, when I walked in the door. They knew I had not slept but, more important, that I was in the battle for my life.

THE WRITING BEGINS

The world is making its giant transformation ... it has never been experienced before and will never be experienced again. It is within the moment, and it is implosive and explosive at the same time. The flower is emerging.

—The Immortal Now

That evening, Kip made the most off-the-wall suggestion I had ever heard.

"Patty, I want you to try something. I know it will sound strange, but my mother has been reading about it."

Kip's mother, Dorothy, was a very bright, loving woman who was the stable source of inspiration for her whole family and her community in Altadena, California. Dorothy had spent a lifetime seeking the divine in the human and was remarkably competent beyond her gentle demeanor. The private side of her life had been a crisscross woven pattern of attending churches like Christian Science while reading everything from the Tao to Jane Roberts' *The Coming of Seth*. Her husband, Harry, had become enmeshed in Scientology, and although Dorothy had supported whatever her husband sought, she also had a practical side, and to her, Scientology was simply too expensive.

"Okay, Kip, whatever you say."

What I meant was, I just didn't care. If he told me to run in front of a bus, I would have done it. In spite of my concern for my children and my helplessness to stop what they were enduring, the ongoing absorption in the "white light" was filling every corner of my life.

"Patty, I want you to try automatic writing. Maybe you'll get some answers to what is going on for you."

"Right."

"No, I mean it."

"Fine."

Then there was a long pause.

"Kip, fine. I'll try anything. How do you do automatic writing? I don't mean to put your idea down, but it's not something people do every day, and I don't believe I had that in school."

"I know. I know. Mother says that you have to envision a white light first, then holding a pen, just rest your hand on a piece of paper, and let it move. Don't lead it; just let it do whatever it wants you to do. If it says something intelligible, just find out what it has to say."

"Okay. Right. Just find out what it has to say."

Another long pause.

"I have a question, Kip. what is 'it' that is talking?"

"Don't know."

"Oh, that helps."

"No one really knows, Patty. It could just be your subconscious. I don't know. Mother said that it helped her, and I respect her, you know."

We all did, so I decided that if it worked for Dorothy, it might help me as well.

That night, I followed Kip's instructions, and the writing began right up. I may have been the most surprised person on the planet. I let out a yelp when the pen started to move. It simply took over, and my hand followed wherever it led. It was very serious and began its story right away. I was fascinated and spent almost the entire night involved with the messages that were coming through. Every time the writing presented an idea I liked and I tried to write my own thoughts, the pen would stop until I let it lead again. It was like dancing with a confident partner who would not let you do any of the leading.

The messages were nothing short of amazing to me. The writing explained right away why I was in such emotional pain and why Robert had done such a terrifying thing to me. It took on the role of a caring parent, and to my amazement, it began leading me out of the valley of the shadow of death. Had I been at any other point in my life, I would have shunned both the idea of automatic writing and Kip for some time, but I was struggling to find a reason to live just one more day. Now I, being born again, began the most important journey of my life.

OTHER LIVES, OTHER LOVES

*When you meditate, you are at one with our existence ... It
exists within its own natural state, but when you allow the
dream to take over and control your existence, then all of the
illusion that creates pain, that creates sorrow, that creates
fear, seem to be in the way of this flow, of this truth,
of the nature of your own being.*

–The Immortal Now

I had never been a believer in reincarnation, but the first thing
the writing said was that this was just one plane of existence
and that the roles that were being played by me and those
around me were carryovers from another life. My relationship
with Robert, it said, was a very old one. It said that not everyone believes in reincarnation because many have never experienced this plane of existence before. I had only twice.

It said that Robert had been a theological student in the
later Middle Ages. I was married at the time to the individual
who was my mother in this life. I was much younger than my
husband and a "young spirit," but very spiritual, and at the time
very beautiful. When Robert met me, he fell in love immediately, much as he said he did when we worked together in Yellowstone Park in this life. We saw a great deal of each other at
that time and, in an unguarded moment, had become passion-
ately involved. I became pregnant, and when my husband, now
my mother in this life, heard about the relationship, he became
completely enraged and killed me. Robert could not survive
the grief and died young.

My husband avoided being brought to justice through the aid of two of his best friends. Those friends came back in this life as my mother's brothers, Wyman and Swede. My father, in my previous life, was a minister, and he tried the rest of his life to prove my husband's guilt with no success. My father came back in this life as my sister, Gretchen.

The writing said that we had all come back together in this life to work out that relationship and that my mother had to give me life since she had taken it away before. The remarkable thing about the story was that if you knew the people involved, it would all fit.

My mother was very close to those two brothers, and whenever she did not want to face anything, even with her own children, she would say that she was going to tell Wyman and Swede what was going on, and they would take her side.

My sister, Gretchen, had been on a lifelong crusade for the truth—to the point of turning others against her. It was an obsession. And then there was my relationship with Robert. Who would have ever believed in love at first sight?

I finally awoke late the next morning and told Gretchen and Kip what had happened.

Gretchen was especially surprised.

"I was your what?" she asked.

"You were my father. But when you really think about it, Gretchen, you have been inordinately protective of me, and you know that quest for justice you have."

"But, Patty, I am your big sister."

"Not that big and not by much." (She is two years older than I.)

I told them how skeptical I was, but I was going to try the writing again tonight anyway.

"Patty, that is just stupid."

Kip chimed in, "But, Gretchen, it can't hurt anything. Look at her. She is more at peace, anyway."

He was right. I could not wait until the next evening to explore further what would be said through the automatic writing. There were two things going on: first, I was surprised and fascinated at what was being said, and second, I was feeling the only sense of peace I had experienced since Robert declared that he was leaving on May 18, 1980—the day Mount St. Helens blew. The writing was like finding shelter in a terrible storm.

The next night was much like the first, except that the teaching was less specific and more universal. I thought the writing would happen only at night, and I had to wait a long time until I was alone in Gretchen and Kip's living room without distraction.

The automatic writing continued right where it left off, repeating that this was just one plane of existence. Then it surprised me with reading my mind. As it mentioned "planes of existence," I had envisioned the crossing geometric planes I had learned about in analytical geometry in high school.

It replied,

> *This plane of existence is not the plane as you are envisioning in your mind's eye but rather horizontal and vertical and thus the symbol of the cross.*

Then it went on to discuss time, saying that linear time is a construct and that what was actually happening was the present. There is no eternal time. It is not possible. The present is all there is. It is unlimited within the life of the individual. There is nothing else. There is no external reality. The experience we are having is like an image on a mirror.

It repeated that I was a young soul and said that Robert and I were soul mates. It said that soul mates do not necessarily have an easy time or idyllic relationships. Sometimes, one encounters a soul mate that is a teacher by adversity. However, the sexual relationship is heightened. It said, reading my mind, that the young spirit was not what I thought. It was an energy, not a time.

It said,

In soul-mate relationships, it does not really matter who is male and who is female. The Tarzan vs. Jane relationships are more for those who do not have a soul-mate relationship, thus the distinct male and female roles are intensified.

The writing then said that what had happened to me was so I could fulfill my own destiny.

It said I would use the writing for guidance and be led to make money for the books I needed to write in my life.

It went on to say,

Many of the things individuals pursue in this life were decided long before they come to the earth. The earth is a school that the individual chooses for specific lessons. Those lessons that are essentially spiritual in nature are not easily defined with the language you use since so many of your words are geared to the experience here and not the larger picture of the spirit.

It said,

For example, your journey has much to do with truth, which is a general term but still recognizable.

That really grabbed my attention since, in so many of my relationships, the central theme had been a search for truth and truthfulness in myself and in others.

I assumed that the books were to be the ones I had researched. My grandfather on my mother's side had built one of the first two buildings in Bridger, Montana, a saloon frequented by Calamity Jane and Bill Cody. I had researched five of the families that had settled the Pryor Mountains and Clark's Fork Valley in Montana in the late 1800s and wanted to write their stories—especially from the point of view of the women involved. So the writing would lead me into a position where I could write? Fine. Whatever it said was okay with me.

The writing then said I could write at any time and I would learn to use "the white light meditation." It said that in three weeks I would have a job on the North Slope oil fields in Alaska, that I would work there for three months and then go to Jackson, Wyoming, to write the books. It said that I would be carefully led the entire way but I needed to get started the next day.

The next morning, I told Gretchen and Kip what the writing had said about the work, the books, and the guidance. I thanked them for my stay, packed the car, and left that afternoon for Jackson, Wyoming. I had pulled money out of my teacher's retirement for travel in Europe and still had some of it left. It was a good two days' drive to Jackson, and forgetting what the writing had told me, I drove during the day, rented a motel, and explored the messages in the evening.

I called Chris, who was still in the hospital in London, and Tim, who was back with his dad, to get updates on how things were going. Chris was healing slowly. I sent a huge batch of chocolate chip cookies I had made at Gretchen's during the day and some souvenir St. Helen's ash. Chris quipped on our transcontinental phone call that when he received the cookies, he felt like the proverbial mosquito in a nudist colony. He knew what to do, but not where to start.

Walter and I decided that Chris would stay with him in Virginia after he got out of the hospital to continue healing and return to the better school he had attended the year before. Then I settled in for a restful sleep.

Messages Become Amazing

The heart has longed for this for a very long time. The heart is like the center of the individual within the present time. It is where life occurs, so when one discovers what life is all about, one goes within the heart.

–The Immortal Now

The second night I arrived in Jackson, Wyoming, and pulled over just outside of town to ask the writing for direction. If I were questioning the validity of the writing—and I always was—I became a believer when it gave the next instructions:

> *You will now go to the Silver Dollar Bar, and you will find a person who will have the house you will live in while you write the books. It will be a man, and you will get his name and phone number.*

I parked the car in downtown Jackson and obediently went into the Silver Dollar Bar. The music was blaring, light glimmered darkly off the varnished log walls, and the room was crowded except for an empty stool at the bar. I took it.

There was a woman seated to my right and a blond, friendly man to my left. I do not remember the pretense by which I wrote down his name and phone number, but I did as I was told, then left. Out in the night air, I told myself that I must be crazy. This stranger could not have a house that I would live in after I came back from my theoretical job on the North Slope of Alaska that I would get in three weeks, but I kept the name and address and found a motel.

The next morning, I had an urge to try the writing during the day. By then, the writing had taken to drawing elaborate pictures that were barely recognizable until they were almost finished. After the pictures were drawn, the description written of them all made sense. So the writing began, and a half hour later, a picture was done.

I began to ask questions. I would write them down and then the writing would respond. Out of the blue, in the middle of an answer to a relationship question, the writing told me to go to Wilson, Wyoming. I looked at the map and found that Wilson was a small town six miles outside of Jackson. I drove out to this charming little western town and passed a particularly pretty log house on a side street. I pulled the car over to continue with the writing process. It said:

The house that you liked is the house owned by the man at the Silver Dollar Bar. You will not make an offer on the house until August 15, at which point you will offer $400. You will move in October 1.

Now that was getting specific: the man at the Silver Dollar Bar owned the house I had just been led to by the writing? I tucked the information away.

One of the most remarkable things about the entire experience was that I followed what the writing said. I didn't believe at the time that the events predicted in it would happen, but when I was writing, I felt comfort. When I was not writing, all I experienced was pain.

Then the writing said,

Your work in Jackson is finished. You wish to see your mother, and you may, but you can only stay for one day because you will need to return to Alaska for the job you will get on the North Slope [oil fields].

My mother lived in Red Lodge, Montana, a day's trip through Yellowstone from Jackson. I arrived in that quaint community nestled at the foot of the massive Rocky Mountains the next day.

There is something about hugging your mother after going through a great trauma. My mother was about five-feet-seven-inches tall and of average weight; a vivacious redhead with peppered white hair, and a certain comforting smell that felt warm and good. They say that baby animals can identify their mothers by their smell, and I felt no different. I knew my mother and could have recognized her hug with my eyes closed. Her body was frailer than mine but with a certain tensile strength that said she was my anchor. I told her that I only had one day with her and that, finally, I really wanted to learn how she made such great pickles.

Without further ado, we zipped the twenty-eight miles over to Bridger, Montana, to gather the famous Clark's Fork cucumbers and dill. We pickled the entire evening, talking and working. I took my pickles with me for Gretchen, whom I would see on my way to Seattle. Then I would make arrangements to catch a plane for Alaska.

Before I left for Bridger, Mom went uptown on an errand. I turned to the writing. It said that I needed to learn the "white light meditation" it had discussed earlier. I listened. All I had to do was lie back, deliberately exclude in my mind's eye any sounds like the refrigerator running or the wind, and to close my eyes and envision a light. It said that I did not have to actually see a light. I could envision what it looks like as the sun comes in through a window. It did not have to be complicated— more like an intention. I would not be gone long, it said, so I didn't have to worry about my mother coming back. It would only take fifteen minutes. I relaxed, and fifteen minutes later, I awoke refreshed—that easy—just as the writing had predicted. I tried to stay an extra day, but it was as if there were a time frame for what was to happen. I left as directed and drove to Seattle with a brief detour to Gretchen's to drop off the delicious homemade pickles, much to her surprise and joy. Two days later, I flew to Anchorage.

On the plane, I asked the writing where I would stay. It responded that I would be welcomed at Kay's house for two-and-a-half weeks until the job on the North Slope materialized. I balked. I barely knew the woman. She was owner and editor of the *Anchorage Daily News*, and the only way I was acquainted with her was that my son, Chris, had been a student of hers in Sunday school. In addition, Kay had a certain status in the world. She had once been married to *the* Marshall Fields and married again to the owner of the *Anchorage Daily News* who had passed away.

Her stepdaughter, Judith, and I were good friends, but I hardly knew Kay. She was a wonderful woman but not a close acquaintance. Now I was supposed to call Kay and ask to stay with her for a significant length of time while a theoretical job on the North Slope materialized? This was almost too much for the complete act of faith in which I was engaged. I argued with the writing, but it simply said, "You will see that it will be all right."

I called Kay's number. My friend, Judith, answered the phone. I told her what had happened and what was occurring now with the writing.

"Great," she replied.

"Great?"

"Yes, Pat. Kay is out of town for the next three weeks, and I'm housesitting while she's gone. I would love the company. Please come right over."

One proof down, five hundred to go!

The writing had me contact Robert on the North Slope and ask him to get me a job. I was supposed to contact the man who had completely broken my heart? It was a miracle that I didn't balk at that, but the writing was the only thread that was keeping me here anyway. Whatever it said, I chose to do. I called Robert.

To the Oil Fields

You will see that the "New Earth" is simply the earth within.
It is the life within. It is the spirit within. It has never left the
individual. It exists as a concept long before it exists
as a prophecy or message.

–The Immortal Now

In two and a half weeks, the job on the North Slope oil fields in Alaska came through. I had been hired as a member of the Teamsters Union to be a warehouse person organizing machinery parts at the Cold Storage Pad on Construction Camp 1, known as CC1.

Judith took me to the airport to head out for Deadhorse, Alaska. I told her about the Silver Dollar Bar directive and said that it would be hard for me to make that call on August 15. I didn't know how accessible phones would be on the North Slope, and I did not even know if the man at the Silver Dollar Bar owned the house. I asked her to make that call for me. She agreed, and I boarded the plane for the oil fields.

The legendary North Slope cannot be imagined. The region is as flat as a calm ocean with a blue and purple color scheme everywhere: in the clouds, the sky, the terrain, and almost the very air. The summer has sunlight twenty-four hours a day, but even at midday, it has a dark, sullen tone to it.

Plants, which live for this too-brief period of light, are miniature versions of their southern counterparts. If nonhuman life forms can have courage, it must reside in the flowers and plants of the extreme north. The air is so still, so quiet. It is as if everything is holding its breath. You can hear your own sounds—your footsteps crunching in snow, your arms rubbing against your jacket, even your own inhaling and exhaling of frost.

Everything in the landscape blends in except the megalithic boxes the oil field workers live in to protect their vulnerable flesh against the most extreme conditions the earth can produce. While everything else on the North Slope is unprotected, it is the protected ones that remain the most conspicuous against the land.

The oil company school bus dropped me off at my new home, CC1, which was almost an acre of a two-story, rust-colored building housing around four hundred workers, fifteen of whom were female. It had nicely furnished rooms and a large dining room. The food was wonderfully fresh, varied, and delicious. The writing had put me on a vegetarian diet, saying that eventually humanity would become mostly vegetarian, primarily for economic reasons. It was very clear that all life is connected, not just human life.

The North Slope is not a hardship tour, and jobs were coveted. Most people worked twelve-hour shifts with two weeks on and two weeks off. I was making thirteen-hundred dollars a week, which was a lot of money.

The North Slope had pay phones so I spoke with Chris and Tim and sent care packages as often as I could. Chris, who was still in the hospital, told me that his cast had been removed and his muscles had atrophied. I sobbed with sorrow and guilt. Always optimistic, Chris reassured me it was normal and he would make sure that he would exercise so his legs would end up the same and he would lose none of his natural mobility.

Walter had made arrangements for his colleague, Peter Jennings, to take Chris to the airport when he was released from the hospital. Peter checked in periodically with Chris by phone, and Chris was looking forward to a limousine ride with Mr. Jennings. At the last minute, Peter was not able to pick him up, so Walter made arrangements for another colleague with the AP who generously gave Chris a lift to Heathrow.

With Chris returning to the United States, his father breathed a huge sigh of relief. Though Walter and I were divorced, I knew he loved his children and would make sure Chris had care and rehab. Chris was safe, and that was all that mattered.

I was settling into the dorm life at Construction Camp 1 and the routine of my new job, if that is what you can call it in that surrealistic world. In the morning, I drove a whistling, rowdy group of men to work in a school bus. The men reminded me of middle-school wrestlers on their first trip out of town. They flirted and chattered like ducks to and from work. The rest of the day, I organized machine parts for the thousands of vehicles that are used in that totally artificial environment. Surprisingly, I was well suited to my position, being a born organizer. It was the German blood, my mother always said. I liked the people I was working with and kidded the men so that they felt comfortable with me.

Robert called as soon as I arrived. He wanted to see me, but I was terrified of him. My height since junior high school had given me the confidence of never being afraid of anything— except everything I had just been through with him.

After David and I divorced, Robert and I had continued seeing each other. He got me a summer job with his company in Valdez, Alaska, and flew in on the weekends to see me. When I returned to Anchorage that fall to continue working with the Indian Education Program, we lived in the same building. Robert said that he was getting a divorce and that he had sent his wife, Susie, and the girls to Scottsdale. Then he got the apartment right above his for me. We spent most of our time together, and I often wondered why we just didn't live together. We had talked about having a baby and made the decision for me not to use birth control. I missed my period and suspected I was pregnant. Then I started bleeding again, and thought maybe I was not.

At Christmas, Robert flew down to Scottsdale to see Susie and the girls while Tim and I went to Hawaii. I thought Robert was making arrangements for the divorce, but when he returned, something had changed. Then I found out I was pregnant, even though I was bleeding. When I told Robert, he said he thought I should get an abortion. I was completely confused. He told me he would give me a few days to make my decision.

I decided to have an abortion as I was still bleeding and thought that something must be wrong with the baby. Also, Robert had changed, I was a professional and a role model for kids, and I was worried about the impact on my sons of my having a child out of wedlock. Here I would be pregnant, without a husband, living with my son, Tim. When I looked at it all, I agreed with Robert and thought an abortion was my best option.

Robert began traveling a lot. Though he said he would be there for the abortion, he was not. Then, one day, he said he wanted to talk to me. That is when he said that our whole relationship had been for revenge, all because I had turned him down when he had asked me to marry him eighteen years ago. That was the day he moved out of his apartment, told me he had bought a new house in Idaho for Susie, and left for his new job on the North Slope. He never returned.

The hypocrisy, deceit, and cruelty of that situation repulsed me. I ached for the comfort of his arms around me, his closeness, and the rhythm of his breathing—everything I had grown to need for my own survival, but I faced an insurmountable wall between us. What I wanted most of all was the return of my illusions about what the relationship was. That had been shattered. Now all I could feel was the fear of his power over me and the pain of his rejection. I only wanted to see him to ask him why he had deliberately hurt me as he had and why he had lied.

Alone in my Construction Camp 1 dorm room, my only comfort was the writing. I wrote and sought guidance whenever I was not working my coveted twelve-hour days, seven days a week.

On August 16, 1980, I received one of the most remarkable calls of my life. It was Judith Hunt. She was shaking as she said,

"Patty, you are not, just *NOT* going to believe this. I called that man in Jackson, Wyoming, as you said."

I had completely forgotten about the August 15 call.

"Thank you, Judith, for remembering."

"Patty, I don't believe it myself. Are you sitting down?"

I replied that I was. I was in one of the phone booths on the Slope that had a small triangular bench in it.

"Patty, the man from the Silver Dollar Bar that the writing directed you to does own that house you saw in Wilson, Wyoming. It is his house, and he uses it as a rental. And there is more."

That alone was enough for me.

"Patty, he said that he was surprised by my call."

He was surprised?

"He said that the people who were renting the house had given their notice just three days ago and told him that they would be moving out at the end of September. Good God, Patty! Can you believe this? He had had no chance to advertise the house for rent, yet, and no one else knew that the current renters were giving their notice, and then I call and offer four hundred dollars per month and say you want to move in October 1!

"Get this, the rent was three-hundred-ninety-dollars a month. The writing was ten dollars a month off. Man, you are sitting at a job that you didn't have three weeks ago that the writing predicted. Isn't that enough?

"I didn't tell you at the time you got the job, but I thought to myself, 'Judith, there must be something to this writing thing!' But now this. Listen to me. Have you ever thought of playing the lottery with this writing stuff?"

There was a long pause.

"Patty, I am shaking!"

She was shaking?

TIME TO GO

Life is expanding. Life is ascending. Life is seeking its own nature. Life is reaching for the love that exists within much as a child reaches for the parent, with open arms. It is joyous.

–*The Immortal Now*

It was almost like walking through a dream someone else had created for me. The pieces all fit. Who could not believe the writing after all of the predictions had come into being in less than a month? The Source had proved entirely credible and nurturing.

In retrospect, I should have just stopped, sung in gratitude that Love was with me, and given everything to a higher power that was guiding me so completely. "Yea, though I walk through the valley of the shadow of death. Thou art with me." I had come to think that *this* life was the valley of the shadow of death—where death was not real, but a shadow that people believed to be true.

I paid the first month's rent for the log house in Wilson from the North Slope and made arrangements, courtesy of CC1 pay phones, to ship my Alaska household goods from storage in Anchorage to Seattle. Then I reserved a U-Haul truck near the Seattle docks to carry all of my earthly goods and Tim's to our new log home in Jackson, Wyoming. There I would be writing books, according to the guidance.

I had researched my mother's family and their trek out West in the 1880s and was loaded with information and interviews. I thought that I was to write their story so it would not be lost to future Zachary family members. I did not notice that the writing said only books and not what kind.

Chris was back in Virginia, living with his father where he could return to the excellent private school he had attended the previous year. Tim had started school briefly in Virginia, but he wanted to return to the West. He had gotten into ski racing in Alaska and wanted to pursue his dream—to become a world-class downhill ski racer. As a talented, bright athlete who was born for speed, Tim had a shot at the Olympics, given the right circumstances, and Jackson Hole was a premier ski-racing town. He also told his father, "Dad, you do not need me. Mom does."

Then the most remarkable thing happened. The writing suggested it was okay to see Robert! It said I would not know how it was to work out but that it would.

Robert kept contacting me. He wanted to see me and explain things. When I finally did meet with him, he told me that he never meant the revenge comments. He was trying to buy time to make sure that his wife and the girls were okay. And once again, he said he would be with me. Robert had gone back to the argument that we were really in love, but the timing had been wrong for us. I was conforming to my romantic dream of how reality should be—that I would be a wife and mother with my sons in a nuclear family. I was simply trying to avert pain.

It should have sounded all too familiar. I fell for the lines of a truly skillful manipulator in spite of masses of evidence to the contrary. I went back into a sexual relationship with Robert, ignoring that he had chosen to leave me six months earlier.

Then, the writing said it was time to leave the Slope. I finished my job on the North Slope and left—simple as that. I gave my two weeks' notice obediently, told Robert who accepted it matter-of-factly, and I believed what Robert said, that he would be coming to Jackson as soon as he could.

I told the men I had taken to work each day in the yellow school bus that I was leaving. They lifted their heads to the sky and howled like wolves, the Prudhoe Bay howl we called it, "Ow, Ow, Ow, OOOOoooo!" The wolf-like chorus probably frightened an innocent white fox or wandering caribou. It was their way of saying good-bye to one of the few women in their lives.

I packed and took another yellow school bus to the Deadhorse airport and boarded the plane with the other workers returning to their homes and families or heading off to blow their hard-earned money in Hawaii. I was going to Seattle to meet Gretchen and pick up Tim, who had been staying with her in Idaho, and then drive to Jackson, move into a pre-ordained house to write books on the West, and wait for the man I loved to return to me.

When I saw Tim at the airport, I was beside myself I was so happy. It felt like "home." Tim, then in the eighth grade, helped me load our earthly belongings from an overseas storage crate into a U-Haul truck. Tim was up for the whole adventure and was looking forward to the Jackson ski slopes. I struggled with a queen-sized mattress, balancing it on my back as it shifted around and almost fell.

"Give me a hand," I said to Tim.

He responded heartily with a round of applause. "Go, Mom. Go Mom! Go! Go! Go!"

"Thanks a bunch, honey!"

The trip was fun. We stopped at Craters of the Moon Park in Idaho. It is a timeless volcanic landscape that has been canonized into a national park. I remember the image of Tim coming down a basalt slope on his bike: the almost-orange symmetrical slope, the thirteen-year-old discovering a form thousands of years old, the sun, and the sense of freedom. There were moments when the world seemed normal and I could escape the entire story my life was playing out.

JACKSON, WYOMING

That which is true permeates everything. It permeates trees.
It permeates animals. It permeates plants. It permeates
humans. It permeates the sky. It permeates the moon. It is
important for you to understand that that which is true
cannot, under any circumstances, be contained within
any religion, within any given scientific theorem, within
any given personal vendetta, personal power system. It is
unlimited, always; therefore, there is no situation in which
one individual has a monopoly on the truth. It is in all
beings, at all times, in all places.

–The Immortal Now

We pulled into the bustling tourist town of Jackson, Wyoming, at about five in the afternoon and headed to nearby Wilson on the main highway, taking the community street, which winds through town and back again in the shape of a *C*. Then we turned onto a dirt drive to our charming home. Finally, we had arrived.

Wilson, located at the base of Teton Pass, was surrounded by the towering beauty of the Teton Mountains. The buildings were old and made of logs. A red elementary school complex anchored the town, and a robust fly-fishing stream busily ran as fast as it could through its center. It was a place of peace where one could either live privately or become reasonably involved with the community. And there in the middle of Wilson, someone I did not know had built my sanctuary. I had been brought to it miraculously through my greatest grief, by a Power I could not fathom, to do a work I could not understand. When I looked at my new home with the sun momentarily breaking through the clouds, I felt the unlimited love of the guidance I was receiving.

Our two-bedroom log house had a front porch extending its length. The living room, with its cathedral, open ceiling, was separated from the kitchen by a small partition. It had new rust-colored carpeting on the floor. The first thing I did was hang up my rust, green, white, and peach Lone Star quilt that had hung in my log house in Chugiak.

The word cozy applied to my new nest—cozy and comforting. But the best part was the small river behind the house. Outside the back kitchen door, the Wilson stream sang its own song 24/7, fifteen feet from the house. When I would walk outside and look up from the stream, I could see the Teton Mountains seeking the sky. The stream music and the mountain and sky panorama played all of the time as Tim and I slept and then awakened in the morning. It sang during the day, and in the evening, it danced with the full spectrum of massive color playing its infinite variety above and around our new home in unbelievable sunsets. It was ironic that I had been led in my grief to a home almost like the one I had left in Chugiak, Alaska, complete with logs, stream, and mountains.

Now, would the guidance lead me to that promised person who would help me write these mysterious books? Who knew? But I was still alive, I had been led thus far, my little family had a precious home, and the guidance had been uncannily accurate.

THE NEW SCHOOL

*It is important to understand that the life that you experience
is connected to all other life and that continuum is the
permanent nature of presence, of the timelessness of the
peace, of the joy, of the love that, in Biblical terms,
"passes all understanding."*

—The Immortal Now

Tim enrolled in school right away. He was three months into the eighth grade, and fortunately, he had been born with social skills. He looked at entering a new school as a challenge. After the first day, he came home and said, "Mom, this looks like a piece of cake."

I was surprised but knew Tim had always gotten along with others even in the worst of circumstances. I had taught on the Makah Indian reservation on the coast of the westernmost point of Washington State where a fellow third grader, David, punched Tim in the arm so often it was generally bruised. Yet, David, somehow, considered Tim to be his friend.

"You know, Mom, even on the first day of school, I have a strategy. I can see where the cliques are and where I need to go."

"A strategy?" I said incredulously.

"I really think I could write a book on the subject," he replied, "a book for eighth graders only—one on teenage group dynamics by a teenager. I think it would work. They were really looking me over."

"That is to the good, honey. You are cool."

"Yep."

End of conversation.

We found his skiing coach, Fred, and Tim joined the Jackson Hole Ski Team as he had hoped. He was talented as a skier and learned quickly. Skiing reinforced Tim's chosen place in the school, so I felt comfortable that the year would prove to be a good one for him. But he worried about his mother, in spite of everything I did to mask what I was going through. He should have.

THE BOOKS FIND A SETTING

The world is ready to see the entire picture. The frustration, the anger, the separateness, the lack of continuity for so many have become intolerable at this point. They seek that which exists within more than at any point in any history, anywhere. And they see the other side.

−*The Immortal Now*

It should have been easy. It should not have involved grief. I was like someone who had been saved. The fairy tale should have happened at that point—the sinner was saved, redeemed, reformed, and the process should have gone on in the same dream-like holograph that had occurred before Robert, before the accident, before the automatic writing. So what was happening?

Robert called when he was on the North Slope, but there was always a reason why he could not come to Wyoming to be with me—a meeting, a trip, or another work obligation. And, he didn't say that he loved me. I began to realize that he was distancing himself from me and said so. Then he would get defensive and say, "I've gotta go." Our calls were short.

The more he called, the more I realized I was dead wrong about him. He had not changed. What he said and who he was were two different things. He was just trying to keep what he had: his wife and kids, the relationship with me at a distance, his money, and the freedom to come and go as he wanted. The cold, frightening destruction of an illusion was coming in like a north wind. I could not face it.

I could function. I knew that. I could get up in the morning, fix breakfast for Tim, and send him off to school making sure that he had his lunch money. I had a cute home and enough savings to get by while I wrote the books. It was a world built on nothing but faith.

Lovingly, the writing taught that there truly is no past and no future. There is only love in the present time. Well, if that love in the present time was what I had experienced when I died and, having survived, I could not go back there, and there is no future, like my illusion of a life with Robert, except for that outlined by the guidance of writing the promised books, then where did that leave me? My heart would not accept the situation I was in without what I mistook as the love of my life.

Finally, from the safety of the North Slope, Robert said, "It is just not going to work out for us, Pat."

Then I found out that I was pregnant.

Three pregnancy tests later confirmed what the first test said. It was as if they were saying patiently, "Yes, my dear, you are going to have a child."

I was not unhappy with the news. I told Robert, and it appeared that my being pregnant with our child was of little concern to him. As for me, I became determined that this time I was not going to lose our child no matter what happened—Robert or no Robert.

In spite of all of the wonderful guidance and spiritual teaching, I returned to a torturous state of grief, crying as much as four hours a day.

The writing persisted in having me meditate a significant percentage of the day. That was the only place where I was at peace. It was within, and yet, I would not accept my present external reality. I was still trying to find any kind of love and peace in the illusions outside me: in my religious beliefs, in seeking love in my relationship with Robert, in the dream of being a wife in a nuclear family, of being a professional person, and in my desire to be a good wife, mother, and moral human being.

The writing said that my relationship with Robert was my relationship with humanity itself. It said that it was preparing me for the books and that I had been taught a mythology that there was life, death, and heaven. That mythology was simply not true. There is only the present time.

I looked at my experience again, as I had in London, and began to notice that there were many times when I had felt hints of that deep, heart-felt joy I had experienced when I died. When Chris was born, I was in the hospital alone with my beautiful baby in a soft, dimly lit room. Holding my baby felt something akin to the London experience. Tim had the most wonderful hugs, and when he put his little arms around me and told me he loved his mommy, I could feel some of what I felt when I died.

The writing said that whenever I meditated or saw water with light playing on it, I entered that place. Whatever brought that deep, love-filled joy moved me to the present and what it called "the presence of the Presence." I became love just for a moment as I did when I died.

The writing said that there is no dualism in the heart—no good/bad, love/hate, yin/yang. We live on multiple planes of existence here, it said. I began to pay attention to what that meant. I had assumed that when you die you disappear and there would be no life. What I did was move to the heart where all is life.

On a practical level, the writing maintained that I stay on a vegetarian diet. It told me I had to quit smoking since I was pregnant. I had learned to rely on it enough so that when it told me to quit, I quit. It was as simple as that. Withdrawal was more endurable than the emotional pain I was in. Besides, Tim and I had come this far. It was not a good idea to abandon the ship—the loving guidance of the writing—in the middle of the ocean of the uncertainty we were facing, in the storm of my state of overwhelming grief and loss. I was writing and meditating a great deal of the day when I was not crying.

Then one day, I made the most puzzling discovery. I walked outside the back door to look at the Teton Mountains looming so close, so grand, with their overwhelming mass in front of me. I could not feel their beauty! Intellectually, I knew they were beautiful, but I felt nothing.

I had been raised in Montana and in Yellowstone Park and had loved the mountains since I was a small child. Wallace Stegner said that he had the rare privilege of growing up poor in Montana, as well as in Saskatchewan and Utah, and as a result, he developed a relationship with the land. He played in the fields, made dams in the streams, and built forts from weeds. As a child, he was outside the better part of each day. I shared that privilege.

Whenever my family drove south from Yellowstone and turned the corner where the Tetons—the Grand and Mount Moran and their entire family of giants—loomed in front of us, not stopped by anything but meadows, there would be a moment when I would stop breathing. Love for the scene would swell within me. I am sure it happens to everyone, but it would overwhelm me.

Now I stood at the back door of my little house close to the mountains and felt nothing! I was truly puzzled and turned to the writing.

"Why do I not feel anything when I look at the mountains?"

You have entered a plane of existence where you are in both worlds—that of spirit and that of [what is frequently referred to as] the World of Fear. You will stay here as you do the books and will return completely to the plane of existence where you will feel beauty when they are completed. It is of the heart as is all reality.

I flashed back to being washed over completely with the unlimited Love I had felt when I died—when I had left this World of Fear—and cried. In a sense, the writing said I was acting as a translator for the Spirit world at this time:

You will use the light and be guided to the person who will help you write the books. You will use the white light meditation and be at peace.

THE CAYCE MEETING

It is the coming of the new age, the coming of a new period,
the coming of enlightenment universally. It is
a dream of so many for so very long.

—The Immortal Now

I used the white light meditation and thought of being guided to the person or persons who would help me write the books. I was curious about how I would meet such a person in Jackson, Wyoming, but I gave it little thought.

Then after about a month of meditation, prayer, vegetarian dieting, crying, and pure faith, out of the blue, the writing gave specific directions again.

You will go to a Cayce meeting.

I responded with the most obvious question, "What's a Cayce meeting?"

I had no idea. I had heard of Edgar Cayce and loved what was said about him. Edgar Cayce was a world-famous healer. People would write in with problems, and he would go into a trance and provide the cure. But in his waking time, the gift of healing and prophecy was not there.

I had been psychic as a child. It was always in a situation where I could save a life if someone would listen to me. From as far back as I can remember, I had dreams of being in a situation with a volcano. I knew how to save those I loved, but they paid little attention until it was almost impossible to get through the lava flow to help them.

On the morning my father died, when I was ten years old, I turned to my mother abruptly and said, "We cannot go to school today. We must stay with Daddy. He is going to die today if we don't."

My mother was a teacher. My father was working in construction after a disastrous year for him. He had lost his job as the manager of a large resort hotel, the Shore Lodge, in McCall, Idaho. As a born engineer who had made a living in the construction business during World War II, he took a job working for Morrison-Knudsen near Boise, Idaho, and was home for Christmas. At the time, I knew I was being blunt with my mother, but I had to be. I held my fifth-grade ground.

"Mother, we have to stay home."

"Patty, we have to leave now. Harry, are you feeling all right?"

My father replied that he was. He was a little tired; that was all. At fifty-two, he had taken his four children skijoring the day before.

"Patty, he says that he feels okay."

That fall, a heart examination and tests showed that he had an enlarged heart. The explanation, according to 1952 medical thinking, was that his heart was enlarged because he had been an athlete in high school and college. To the doctors of the time, it was not significant.

I reluctantly went to school that day but spent the morning in a cold sweat, panicked with worry. The school was about five miles from our house in downtown McCall. When we went to lunch at Ford's Cafe at noon that day, I forced my mother to call my dad. I remember thinking as she came back to the table, *She will say he's okay, but he isn't.*

"He's okay," she said.

When school was out that day, Mother had a teacher's meeting, and I was supposed to stay at the school and ride back with her and my brother and two sisters. I was normally an obedient child but disobeyed my mother in a desperate attempt to save my dad. I took the school bus home and ran to the house as fast as my ten-year-old legs would carry me.

As I rounded the corner to get to our house, I thought, *It's too late. He's died of a heart attack, just like Dickie Zimmerman's dad died.*

I had no idea what a heart attack was, but when I opened the front door, there was my beloved father, face down. His body was a strange blue color.

I grabbed the phone and could get nothing but the operator. I told her that my father was dead of a heart attack and tore down the alley to the house of a friend of ours who was a nurse. I told her that my father was dead of a heart attack and could she go and check to make sure that I was wrong and that I was going to get my mother. I left her and ran to another neighbor's house and got a ride to school.

I would never have interrupted a teacher's meeting in my life, but I gathered up all of my nerve, burst into the meeting and blurted out what had happened. My mother's face paled, and all the wheels that go into effect in a situation like that began to move in slow motion: my mother went to the house, my siblings and I were carted off to Aunt Eunice's house, arrangements were made, people brought food and said how sorry they were, and life went on.

So when the writing said Cayce, somehow I felt at peace. I did not know much about him, but he just sounded good to me because I was told he was psychic. I really had no idea what that meant. It was not a label that I was concerned about.

I looked up "Cayce meeting" in the phone book, but to no avail. I called Nola, a new acquaintance of mine in Wilson, and asked her if she knew where a Cayce meeting might be. She said she did, that she had been interested in the Cayce works and knew of someone who would know where the meetings were held.

The meeting was Thursday at a house owned by someone in Teton Village named Barbara McCormick. I gathered the seventeen notebooks filled with automatic writing along with my courage and went to the meeting.

As I walked into Barbara McCormick's condo, there was a short hall with the kitchen to the left, a bath downstairs, and one bedroom to the right. Two bedrooms were upstairs. It was a place I would come to know well. The condominium had a two-story open ceiling and a stone fireplace in the living room. There was a walkway on the second floor with a library facing the open living room.

The group of about seven people were gathered and being led by a light redheaded woman, medium build, about five feet eight, in her sixties with a warm smile and welcoming demeanor. She beckoned for me to come in. I just liked her.

She began the meeting and asked why we were there. I am sure everyone has had a moment of hesitation when being put on the spot, but mine was considerably longer. Then I thought, *If you don't tell them, you will have to come back later, plus they will ask about the seventeen notebooks you are carrying. Fine!*

"My name is Patricia Grabow. I've been led to this meeting, and the guidance is long and contained in these seventeen notebooks. I've been told to come to a Cayce meeting, and if I do, I will find someone who will help me write books that I believe are to be about the American West. There, I said it."

Everyone smiled kindly and even looked as if they understood what I had just said. Barbara McCormick looked at me very calmly and then just grinned from ear to ear.

"What has taken you so long? I've been waiting for you!"

THE SOUL MATES

The world as you experience it within the present time is all there is. There is the vehicle by which understanding occurs.

−The Immortal Now

B arbara and I met the next day for coffee at her place. She told me that a year ago at the age of sixty-three she had had major surgery for a hiatal hernia. The doctors had to go in, separate her ribs with the equivalent of a tire jack, repair the junction of the esophagus and the stomach, and sew her back up. Barbara said that she never thought she would live through the damage to her body. When she woke up afterwards, she said to herself, in a surprisingly disappointed state of being, "Oh well, there's something I have left to do here." She had been waiting for a year for me to show up. When I walked into the room, she said that the smile was not just courteous; it was also genuine.

The writing said that Barbara was what is termed a "soul mate," that is, in its expression, a friend in the truest sense of the word.

It said that the idea of soul mate was not quite what is generally accepted in Western thought and that there were traditions on Earth that better understood the concept. The soul mate is a true spiritual relationship, the writing said, which functions on a plane of existence other than the intellectually conscious plane. Soul mates are like water from the same river running down the mountain. The river has much energy, and that energy is derived from its relationship with the mountain—not from the nature of the river itself. The soul mate, it went on, gains its energy from its interaction with the Larger Being but does not lose its own identity. Likewise, the many rivers running down a mountain share many of the same characteristics and encounter similar experiences. However, the Larger Being, like a mountain can, in fact, have many rivers running down it and not lose its own energy.

People with similar characteristics of the heart can be soul mates, and these relationships can create a dynamism in the interaction of several identities. When soul mates gather, healing can occur. It said that we will understand more about soul mate relationships the more we come to an understanding of the kind of Love I felt when I died.

I knew that I felt comfortable around Barbara. I felt at home in her presence, like a joyous child visiting a favorite relative. I looked around her extensive library and was surprised to find an array of books that I would have bought for myself. There was nothing she was interested in that had not been of interest to me at some point. Even her choice of furniture and colors were those I had always loved. It is easy to see why we became such good friends.

It was truly as though she had stayed around here on Earth after her operation and waited for me to show up. She had been.

"Patricia," Barbara said one day, "there is another couple and their family I know you must meet. I am certain of it. Their names are Bruce and Charlotte McArthur, and their children are David, Thomas, and Sue. I've gone ahead and made arrangements for you to meet them tomorrow."

"Okay. Great idea. What did you say their names were?"

"You heard me, dear friend."

Barbara told Bruce and Charlotte McArthur about me and the seventeen notebooks of writings. The McArthurs and Barbara had to be close spiritually. Otherwise, if a couple had been told the story of the my many notebooks filled with the guidance I had received, much less the fact that I had followed that guidance, typically they would have looked at Barbara with a severely jaundiced eye and run, not walked, in the other direction. Not so with Bruce and Charlotte.

Barbara and I met with Bruce and Charlotte. Bruce stood about six feet tall, was slender, in his sixties, with a twinkle in his eye and a warm, engaging, ready smile. Charlotte was pushing about five feet four inches. Bruce, I learned, had been on the board of directors for the Association for Research and Enlightenment and the Edgar Cayce Foundation. He had given lectures and was developing a book on the Universal Laws he found in the Cayce works. Charlotte had researched the Essenes, the religious retreatist group of Jesus's day. She had supported her husband's work in every way and had developed interests of her own. They were open, seeking, loving, and as broad as the Western plains in their thinking. What I was going through was within the normal realm for them, even though it was new to me.

We visited for a short while, and I realized that Barbara was right. I needed to meet these amazing people. They wanted to know every detail of what had happened thus far. The thing that struck me was that in spite of the fact that they had spent a lifetime in prayer and sincere spiritual seeking, they had never reached a place where they "knew" it. They were constant learners.

When I asked if this is what I should be doing, Barbara, Bruce, and Charlotte chuckled and said, "You are. Aren't you?"

Charlotte said more than once, "It is not that we *should* do anything. It is that we *could*, isn't it?"

So my spiritual family was now complete. I had Tim with me. Chris and I spoke frequently, and I felt he was with me in spirit, even though he was back in Washington, D.C. Barbara

McCormick, Bruce and Charlotte McArthur, and their wonderful family were surrounding me with all of the kindness a person could dream of. When I wrote that night, the writing said that Barbara, Bruce, Charlotte, and their family were "soul mates" and that on another level they knew that I was in trouble and had drawn me to them in order to help me.

The writing began to teach how the white light worked. It said,

When you use the light, you create the circumstances into which you walk.

Part of what I was to do was to teach this meditation so that others could use it in the time ahead.

THE BOOK BEGINS:
PASSAGE FROM FEAR

You will see that there is a window within your own being that allows for that transformation. It is nothing you will do consciously. It will not be what you perceive it to be, and it will be beyond all human comprehension.

-*The Immortal Now*

I have always worked hard. My widowed mother believed in the work ethic, and had insisted that her four children learn to work long hours and be thorough. She left two axioms embedded in my mental framework: anything that was worth doing was worth doing well, and you should always leave a place better for having been there. She taught school, supported her entire extended family during the Depression, and later, after my father died, put three of her four children through college.

At the time of my experience in London, I had taught for ten years, worked sixty-hour weeks, and took care of children and family to the point where I had no leisure time. What was leisure time? The only time I had been at home without a job was when Chris and Tim were small and Walter had insisted that I stay home. I was simply not made for that life, not intellectually, and not in terms of skills. Walter loved nothing better than a well-prepared, gourmet meal. I was not fond of cooking at all. My meals were legendary in their screw-ups. Wrong woman.

Then after the events in London and led by the writing, I ended up in Jackson in a beautiful cabin, pregnant, crying half the day, and meditating the other half—hardly productive in the ways I had been taught. In my heart, I was not enthusiastic about outlining the book on the Zachary family, but I was obedient.

I had done some research, had a foggy idea of how a book might be put together, a possible helper in Barbara, and the assurance that the books would start soon. The writing had me meditate frequently, and before I began the meditation, I was told to think of the books starting. Fine.

Then one day out of the blue, the writing said that the books would begin. Hooray!

The writing said to relax and let the books come through the writing process. Well, there it was. My worries were over. I would not have to go through the conscious planning process I was dreading.

So I meditated, and the writing for the book began.

It was definitely *not* a book on the American West. I wrote for over an hour the first day, January 16, 1981. The writing had the same wonderful spiritual messages that were getting me through the roughest part of my life:

> *You will see in this book that the more preponderant force, by far, is the spiritual of which all life is a part. You will also see that the end product is close and being prepared now. You are that product and need to look at the wonders within ... You are the end product, and you are all there is—there is nothing more.*

I was spellbound and let the writing continue. Every so often, I would think a conscious thought, and the writing would stop until I let go of it. Then it would continue with the last word it had given. The process was slow going because of that, but I could not stop. I was surrounded with the same comforting, loving sense I had experienced before. It continued:

> *You may assume that matter is your creator, but you are your creator, in fact, and you have the power to determine your reality. You will look into your past and see an event that you can assume you did not create; for example, a situation in which you felt uncomfortable. You will see that it was one that did not kill. It was only hurtful or uncomfortable.*

> *You will be able to see, now, that it was you who created the situation. The purpose of your creation was the essence of life on this plane, discovering the brink of your limitations but not extending them to the point of no return and that is all death is, a point at which you cannot return to this plane. You are not free, yet, of the limits of matter; for that is part of this plane of existence, which we shall get into later, but you can be free of the brinkmanship that is harmful to either yourself or others—at which point you are in control of this existence. You are the author of the script and will write a good play or a horror story, depending on your frame of thought.*

Then as abruptly as it began, it quit for the day and said I would write again tomorrow. It instructed me to meditate in the interim.

I could not wait to tell my new friends what had happened. I called Barbara, and she was just happy that something had happened. She said that she would call Bruce and Charlotte and told me to call her again tomorrow and let her know if it happened again as it had today. I knew it would.

[January 17, 1982]

Humankind is not prepared to write the script for this time and place. You were a hundred years ago, but the evolution of man, that is, the spiritual evolution, was based on a sense of community that exists no longer. The net result is a sense that the world is not a good place or that people are not good—neither of which is true. The world itself has not changed nor has the spiritual substance of the individual. Those people who were here on earth a hundred years ago were not kinder than those who are here today, just as the animals that were here a hundred years ago are not less swift or capable of surviving in their natural habitat, but the habitat changed, dramatically, and therefore the adaptation is not appropriate. The habitat will change in the next hundred years ten times more dramatically, and you, dear reader, need to be prepared for it.

I was surprised at that statement and stopped momentarily to think about it. I had been good friends with someone labeled a "born-again Christian." I saw her as a dear, serious, strict, kind friend, and she had said that the earth was going to change to where it was almost unrecognizable as we know it. But this text was saying that what we thought were enormous changes were insignificant compared to this period ahead. Millions of books had been sold by those who agreed with my Alaskan friend, Barbara, but this was saying that the changes were in consciousness. It went on.

Your happiness will depend on the adapting you are willing to do. You will see, in time, that you have a unique capacity in the realm of life. You have the capacity to recognize and communicate with the world of the spirit—not spiritualism, for that is confusion and fear, but the spirit that exists within. That spirit will guide you out of the world of illusion into a reality you will only wonder at and say you had no idea it existed, but it has been the substance of Life on this planet since the beginning. There have been good people who have been aware of it and called it God, but, unfortunately, it is more than the various concepts will allow it to be, so, it will remain untapped until you allow yourself the experience of it rather than the reading or the church-going or the sacrifice known as morality. All concepts, even the most expansive, are of themselves limited by their definition, and so the world becomes deluded and separated into factions—all of whom feel their exposure means the whole.

So there it was, the beginning of the first of four books I was to do. There was the result of so much preparation—housing, finance, moving, diet, meditation, prayer, grief—all to come to this point where the vision of unlimited Love I saw when I died could be manifest and come through. Now I knew the books would be more than I could assume in my most expanded imagination.

Then the writing told me to call Barbara, Bruce, Charlotte, and David together, make a copy of the script, and give it to them and ask for their thoughts.

I called Barbara.

"Barbara! It wrote again!"

"It did?"

"Yes! Could you do me a favor?"

"Of course!"

"Could you get Bruce, Charlotte, and their son, David, together. I'm being guided to show all of you the beginning of the books."

I made copies of the script so that they would have a chance to read it and to consider what it had to say. It was tough taking it to them, even though I knew they would understand and welcome whatever happened. It was as though I had, in faith, gone ahead and walked off with a parachute strapped to my back and was not sure that the thing would open. These remarkable four people I had met were that parachute. What they had to say would affect the rest of my life, and I knew it.

We met at Bruce and Charlotte's home at Teton Village. As I drove to their house, the land was blanketed with snow, and the sunlight was reflected from millions of crystals, almost blinding me. It was like my experience in London. The light was entirely of the heart. In a totally different state of being, this time the light was visual, and my heart was pounding rapidly with trepidation. I knew I was surrounded with love, but I was afraid.

The mountains behind Teton Village rise straight up from the valley floor like a giant cathedral wall taking your eye into the clouds and to whatever lies beyond the earth. The drive follows the foot of that impenetrable wall. I turned into where I had been given directions to the McArthur home and pulled in front. It was nestled against the mountains—simple and grand. It seemed like forever as I made my way from my little Toyota truck to that beautiful home where the roofline imitated the peaks behind.

As they answered the door, they gave me a hug. It was their way.

"Patricia, we're so glad to see you. Barbara and David are waiting in the dining room."

"Thank you. Sorry for the short notice."

"No, we're excited about the book!" as she gently ushered me down the hall.

They were welcoming and so kind to me. We walked past a six-foot-tall wooden statue of an angel. It was one with no name. The windows that rose to the top of the cathedral ceilings seemed to take in the entire span of the Teton Mountains above. The light I experienced during my drive was streaming in over the brilliantly white snow, flowing into the windows and filling the room. The home reflected the light and the largess of the owners.

In the dining room where Barbara and David were waiting, there was a sense that there was another dimension to that meeting. To me, they were like gods on Mount Olympus that day. They greeted me warmly and wrapped me in a blanket of love.

I remember them at a table, lined up, seemingly elevated above me, though I knew they were not. They were not dressed in white robes as in a painting, but they seemed that way to me. I recalled a scene from a Superman movie in which Jor-El goes before the council to say that the planet Krypton would be destroyed, and there was white everywhere in the scene— white robes, white light, white background—so that the faces were made even clearer. The context of the scene was not what I saw in my mind's eye, but the presence of the wisdom of those who had grown into such presence spiritually that their advice would be coming from a greater Source.

I snapped out of my awestruck reverie and saw them as they were—loving, caring human beings who were intent on helping me the best they could. To this day, I think what I experienced as I went into that dining room was seeing them to some degree as they really are, at another level. They were smiling, I was drinking tea, and they had much to say.

David, who was a Unity minister, spoke first.

"I read the pages you gave me. They are remarkable. And, to me, what's even more remarkable is how they came into being."

"That's how I see them," Charlotte said gently.

Bruce's eyes sparkled. "I'm actually thrilled with what I've been reading. There's a kind of integrity to the work. I'm looking forward to the whole process, Patricia."

I was relieved and so grateful and felt as if I had moved into the richness these people contained within themselves. There was a sense that we were about to embark on an amazing journey.

They asked questions. We discussed the text itself and the process by which it came, and through the discussion, there was nothing but focus on supporting me and on how they could help. I relaxed and sank into their friendship like a child.

Charlotte was always checking in, seeing if we would like something to drink and if we were comfortable. She was concerned about the well-being of those who entered her loving sanctuary. We drank herbal tea and basked in the sunlight and each other's company that afternoon. I was with those whom I would grow to love with all of my heart.

Now, How Exactly Do You Do This?

So that, if you are in the presence of love, you are at one with love. There is no time involved. If you are in the presence of a friend, you are with a friend at some level. It is not important that you think in terms of a moment with a friend.

–The Immortal Now

One of the topics during our brief discussion with the McArthurs was the process by which the message was coming through.

I described what happened when the text came through the automatic writing—how halting it was and, when I became consciously aware of what was being said and began to even slightly analyze it, the message would stop, wait, and then begin again when I relaxed. It was a lengthy process, and I was concerned about it.

Through Bruce and Charlotte's association with the Cayce Foundation, they knew many people who had channeled works. Among them was a person called Lama Sing in Florida and another one was in Seattle. Bruce suggested that I go to the person in Seattle to learn about what was called "voice communication." It was all news to me, but I was open to whatever I was led to.

It was going to be difficult to come up with the money for the trip and whatever fee I might be charged, as well as leaving my son Tim. He relied on me for transportation to and from school and skiing, so I would have to make arrangements with others. Barbara said that she would be willing to help out. She lived about five miles north of Wilson. Bruce, Charlotte, Barbara, and I discussed the subject back and forth for about a week, looking at the particulars, the details of the trip, and what it all might entail.

I was learning fast. To Barbara, Bruce, and Charlotte, works produced through experiences like mine and others at the Cayce Foundation were all part of their life. I had read the series of *Seth Speaks* books by Jane Roberts but never wondered how they happened. What was the process? My doing the channeling was just part of what others were doing on a larger scale. It was as though I was trying to write sentences leaving out pronouns and transitions and not even knowing what was missing.

Time passed. I was still meditating frequently and much of the day. The baby in me was growing rapidly and simply was not a passive person in any way. The baby was a kicker. I was doing the automatic writing for comfort and guidance and was busy being a mother. January, February, and then March passed. The grief was omnipresent since Robert called periodically. I would almost forget what was happening, and then he would call and suggest a possible future scenario.

My mother stopped taking her high blood pressure medication and was placed temporarily in a nursing home. My sister who lived in Laurel, Montana, called and asked me if I could bring mother to live with me in Jackson while she recuperated. I agreed and drove to Red Lodge, Montana, in the winter, picked up her and her baggage, and returned to Jackson. My mother needed a great deal of care at first. I had to bathe her, feed her, and tend to all of her needs. It was a real opportunity for me.

I had always been very close to my mother. She, if the writing was correct, had a great love for me as well. This remarkable, independent woman was helpless, probably for the first time in her life. She still had her wonderful wit about her. Her body was just temporarily frail.

Slowly, she gained strength with the careful feeding and full-time care I was offering. I was still doing the writing and meeting with Barbara but would go off in my room to do so. My mother was sharing Tim's room, which was not easy for an eighth grader, but necessary. Tim's room was large with a vaulted ceiling so it had a wonderful sense of space.

Mom was with us a little over a month before she was back on her feet and anxious to get back to her lovely two-story Victorian home in Red Lodge. My sister and I made arrangements for her to spend some time there but to move her to a retirement home in nearby Billings so she could get the care she needed.

After taking Mom to Billings, I went back to trying to figure out how to take the next step with the books.

THE BOOKS BECOME EASIER

The love that is there binds all life to all life. It is nothing that is new. It is nothing that is discovered. It exists.

—The Immortal Now

The problem was solved more easily than any of us could have imagined. One day after all of that prayer, faith, and meditation, the message simply came through the writing.

It said that it would not be necessary for me to go to Seattle or anywhere for the voice communication. It gave specific instructions. Barbara and I were to go to her place. I would lie down, use the white light meditation I had been taught, and the book would continue. It said that Barbara would be with me at each session and that she would turn on a tape recorder whenever I began to speak and turn it off when the speaking stopped. Easy, clear, and to the point.

I called Barbara first to tell her the news. I could tell that she was pleased and slightly insecure at the same time. She had no experience with this. This woman who had been around the world untold times and had traveled one-hundred-thousand miles by air the year before she retired to Jackson, who had run entire departments, who was the epitome of worldliness, was slightly nervous but willing to try whatever she was told. She and I become very close.

Then I called Bruce and Charlotte. I remember that Bruce laughed as only he could. He would throw his head slightly back, and a light laugh would emerge from all of him—his eyes, his smile, and his very nature. Charlotte was happy, and in her gentle way, she said, "Well, of course."

So it was set. Tim was off to a ski race with friends. We made arrangements for a tape recorder and to do the session in Barbara's condominium.

Barbara's home was a reflection of the entire planet Earth—a microcosm of the macrocosm. Barbara always said that she felt the Tetons were one of God's acupuncture points. There was a sense of the Divine in that place, no matter where you went in the Jackson area.

The condominium was decorated in earth tones with Barbara's extensive collection of memorabilia from all continents: Africa, the South Pacific, the Orient, the Middle East, and Europe. She had sparkling, interesting things collected from a lifetime of travel, reading, exploring, writing, and celebrating life in every form that can be found by a single person. Her condo was a museum, a library, a home, and a cathedral all wrapped into one place where we were beginning a remarkable part of our journey together as friends.

After our conversations, I found out that I actually had met Barbara my senior year in high school in the South Pacific! She taught at the same school I had graduated from on the island of Guam, Tumon Junior/Senior High School, and had lived only five houses—Quonset huts, actually—away.

Barbara had prepared for our session. There was a large couch in front of the two-story stone fireplace, and the tape recorder was set up, per the writing's directions.

I lay down and began the white light meditation as I had been instructed. The book, the writing said, would just continue from where it had left off after the sixteen pages.

The text for the book streamed out of me. Barbara's voice was also caught on tape:

"Oh, my gosh! Is the tape recorder on? Oh, yes, I see a light. It's on! Oh, my gosh!"

She apparently was jumping around the living room like a rabbit desperately wanting to make sure that nothing went wrong as a steady stream of text came from me.

And I? I was in another world, and apparently the words were coming forth, picking up from where they had left off. It was as though I had been lifted up to another plane emotionally when I went into the meditation, and it was illuminated.

I was conscious that the words were coming out of me, but I was entirely focused on staying out of the process and letting it happen. It was like walking a tightrope and being careful not to step off, with the whole purpose, somehow, to set aside my conscious mind, my beliefs—me in any form taken on in a lifetime—and just let this message come through.

During that time, I was in a state of pure love and felt surrounded with the same kind of love I had experienced when I died, but to a lesser degree. It was the same kind of love I felt when listening to music or being "in love" or watching the sun come up over the mountains. It was peace in the form of love.

The meditation session lasted about twenty minutes and produced continuous text for the first book the entire time. Then it stopped. Barbara said afterwards that my voice was very soft, but clear and comforting, and she was excited as she listened to what was being said.

I slowly returned after the words stopped. I took deep breaths, stretched, and opened my eyes to see Barbara's face above me filled to overflowing with curiosity. She was almost in tears and anxious to tell me what had happened from her perspective.

"Pat, it worked! Did you hear what it said? What happened to you? Oh, my gosh, it worked! You became so peaceful, and then you just started talking. Wow! I can't believe this is happening."

When I "came back" after the nineteen minutes, all I knew was that I was pretty tired out and very cold. Later, Bruce and Charlotte said they had forgotten that I should be covered up during the session because the body temperature can drop dramatically. They also told me to take high quantities of Vitamin C to help deal with the stress during this process.

I could hardly lift my eyelids and could not move, but I was elated.

"Barbara, I'd appreciate a cup of coffee."

As she brought me the coffee, I sat up slowly. The coffee felt warm, and I began to talk to a very curious friend.

"I have to know, Pat," Barbara said, "what happened for you? Where did you go? How did you know what to say? Do you know what was just said? It was wonderful!"

"Pat, it used the word 'God.'"

That seemed completely natural to both of us. Neither one of us had ever thought that it was not possible to communicate at all times with God, whatever one thought that to be. It was like breathing. Both of our homes were filled with books that affirmed our closeness with God as described in an untold variety of ways, and the idea was welcomed in a very simple way.

I told her that I could only hear bits and pieces of what was being said and that the words almost sounded like an echo in a large room and that my entire efforts had gone just to getting out of the way and letting everything happen as it must.

We wrapped me in a blanket to warm up. I really needed to remain quiet and just relax. Barbara did all of the talking. She described more of what happened for her and played back the tape for me.

To our surprise, the writing had picked up from where it had left off from the previous session as though there were no time in between.

The Daily Schedule

*You will see that what theologians have called the "Presence
of God" is the only existence there is. It is not that God is in
our lives. It is that Presence is within the individual.*

–The Immortal Now

We made the decision to meet as often as we had energy,
mostly at Barbara's place. Tim was in school all day,
and since Barbara was retired, there would be time, so we met
the next day. The session began with comfort for me regarding Robert. It said that I would begin to understand why the
relationship had happened as it had and that it would work out
with Robert in ways I could not understand. At the time, of
course, I thought that meant he would return to me, but it was
never phrased that way. The Source knew so much more than
I did but understood me at the same time. After the comfort
given in the session, it went right into where it had left off the
day before.

It went on for about twenty minutes and spoke of this
being one plane of existence and that, in any given second, we
functioned on literally thousands of planes. It explained that
we were in an "inarticulate consciousness" as long as we were
here, that so much of our lives were so complex that they could
not be reduced to words. It did not limit itself to human life
and consistently included all life in its discussion.

We met daily once the book began. I was well into my sixth
month of pregnancy, and as all pregnant women and couples
know, there are frequent trips to the bathroom. Not that it
interfered, but it did mean that the sessions became shorter

as the book progressed. The baby was very active. It kicked, wiggled, and squirmed much more than my other children had, but when we went into a session, the child was completely quiet and serene.

THE WILSON STREAM

When you become at one with your own being, you see that
there is intrigue, fascination, and unlimited capacity to see
the world in terms of its own true nature. It is like
looking on a field of beautiful flowers.

–The Immortal Now

Our little log house was on the Wilson Stream, a perfect metaphor for my life and the progress of the book as it ran throughout that winter. The snow and ice attempted to cover the water, but the ice was always limited to just the shore and seldom jutted out onto the stream more than a foot.

Wilson Stream was a full, clear little river, and it was remarkable to me how swiftly it ran on its rush to the ocean. I would walk outside in the back yard onto a small layer of snow covering weeds that had been cut to look like a lawn during the summer. Everything crunched under my boots.

I'd watch the Wilson Stream's frenetic journey that seemed so peaceful. It held such purpose, providing necessary nurturing of the life that lay along its path. The stream enveloped the light above it and mixed a color palette that included everything in the water and pierced deep into the green bottom. Aquatic plants swayed softly as the water worked its path to wherever it was meant to go, and I watched the stream's travel with fascination. It was a flow and a journey. I, too, was a flow and a journey, along with Barbara and the McArthurs. We were present. We were light. We, though we were conscious, were unconscious beings—a presence in a Presence.

The ocean was simply the stream's goal, and yet, the ocean and the stream were one. I could feel this connection to the whole, though I could never quite map out the route it was to take. The whole existed as substance and motion. It was like me at that point. I was that stream and was connected to the spiritual whole. I was, like the water, unaware of how I was nurturing life, but the child I was carrying was experiencing it daily. It was real, and it was ancient, and most of all, it was everything I did. I was life, and I, whatever that was, was present breathing, in motion, and we were on our course.

The writing continued daily in Barbara's condo or at my home. When we had sessions at the Wilson house, we could hear the stream faintly in the background of the tape recorder.

Skiing Down the Tetons

You are a being of light. You are a being of love.
That light, that love, does not change.

—The Immortal Now

Barbara, Tim, and I began to see Bruce and Charlotte frequently. They loved Tim and admired his eighth-grade commitment to his mom. Tim was skiing daily, and the ski parents attended every meet, provided support for their kids, and worked together. I became part of that group. It didn't occur to me that, at seven months pregnant and still not showing it very much, I should not be skiing.

At one point, I had taken Tim to race at Sun Valley. He did not want me watching so I skied into the woods to sneak a peek. While I was trying to turn around, I lost my balance and floundered like a beached whale in the snow, alone and very embarrassed. I wondered, remembering the saying, "If a tree falls in a forest, does anyone hear it?" *If a lone pregnant woman skier falls in this forest, will anyone ever hear me?* Somehow, I managed to get up with the assistance of a nearby Aspen and figured that I deserved it for going against my son's expressed wishes. Okay, I won't do that again.

The parents were expected to help, and at another race, they asked me to carry a backpack of canned soda up to the top lift at Teton Village, not realizing I was pregnant. Fine. After I dropped off the backpack, I started to ski down the main course of the mountain, and around halfway to the bottom, Tim schussed up to me. He said, "Mom, watch this."

He took off and all but flew below me, beautifully executing every turn, as Emily Dickinson said in one of her poems, "Too silver for a seam." He was simply not earthbound in any way, like rhythm in motion unto itself and completely free of any limits that might stop his quick turn, flying and returning to earth like a water-savvy seabird skimming across the water and then disappearing into the light at the horizon. I vowed then to do whatever was necessary to keep Tim skiing. He possessed such a gift.

He disappeared, and I continued skiing toward the car when I caught an edge and, unlike my nimble son, I fell, fortunately, in the soft snow. I was not hurt and picked myself up and skied slowly the rest of the way down the hill, but it was the first time I realized that I could hurt the baby I was carrying. That was my last ski excursion until after my child was born.

ENDINGS, BEGINNINGS, FORGIVENESS

You will see that as the earth begins to free itself in the
world of thought from fear-based thinking, it
returns to its natural harmony.

–The Immortal Now

For six weeks, Barbara and I met almost daily for a session, starting April 13 and continuing through May 30, 1981. We produced seventy-four sessions during that time. The writing predicted at the beginning how many pages the book would be, that there would be three sections and twelve chapters. It turned out to be accurate once the first book was published! It also said that other books were being generated, and the first book had four sister works. The Source did not initially name the books except one. The writing also said that I was not to be a visible channel—that the books were to speak for themselves.

What remained so remarkable to me was that the book was a continuous whole. Each day when we'd quit, we would end at the close of a sentence. The next day when we started, the sentence would begin again exactly where it had left off the day before. How did it do that? I have rarely been able to retain something from day to day, so it certainly had nothing to do with my personal consciousness. When we finished the last session for the first book, Bruce and Charlotte suggested entitling it, *The Renaissance: Passage from Fear*.

The baby was very close to due. The ski season was over, so Tim's ski team parents remained unaware of his prospective new sibling, and it was just as well. Love had provided me with a very loving, close, and dear group of friends to welcome this wonderful new person into the world of ours. Barbara became my Lamaze coach, and we took the series of classes together. Barbara was sweet and kind and so very understanding of what I was facing. I trusted her completely and was comfortable with anything she did. I read a book on birth without violence. The baby was to be born at the Jackson Hospital without violence, I had decided, at the new birthing room they had created there.

Robert somewhere, somehow, decided that he wanted to be with me when the baby was born and called from the North Slope. By this time, I had my doubts about whether this would happen since, in my unbiased judgment, that promise was being made by a true, unadulterated, and to-the-core cross between a mean-spirited chicken and a human being!

One day about six weeks before the baby was due, Bruce McArthur announced, while we were visiting, that I would, at some point, have to forgive Robert. *That* was the furthest thing from my mind. As much as I had learned to respect Bruce McArthur, what was he talking about?

"Bruce, that is simply just plain nuts!"

Bruce said that all I would have to do was recite a forgiveness prayer he knew of for forty days. If I missed a day, I would have to start all over again and go forty days straight. Out of wanting to do whatever my dear friend suggested, I listened to his unsolicited forgiveness proposal. I made it perfectly clear that I did not feel forgiving but would consider going through the motions. Bruce said that would be okay. Then he gave me the prayer.

"First you pray to the person you wish to forgive. 'Dear Robert, I am praying to you. Thank you, Robert, for all

*you have done to me. Forgive me, Robert, for doing to
you all I have done to you.'"*

"What? Bruce, are you out of your mind? Let me see, do I
have this right? I am supposed to thank Robert for all he has
done to me? Thank him, my foot!"

Bruce ignored me and said that you then pray to yourself.
*"Dear Patricia, I am praying to you. Thank you, Patricia, for all
you have done to me. Forgive me, Patricia, for doing to you all I
have done to you."*

"Huh? First, I have to forgive him and then myself for
something I didn't do on top of it? I don't think I am the one to
be forgiven. And then, Bruce, you say I have to do this for forty
days? How could this lead to forgiveness and especially for
something I didn't do? Is this what you sincerely had in mind?"

"Yes, Patricia." A true friend, he was deliberately ignoring
any response I had about the prayer.

"You might as well get started today." Then he got ready to
leave.

"Bruce, you know I am obsessed with the fact that Robert
did what he did for revenge."

"Patricia, I am familiar with that. It is not that I am insensi-
tive. I think this needs to be done now and am asking you to
consider forgiveness without having to consciously commit to
it as an option. That's all."

"Forty whole days?"

Bruce's only response was, "Just a minute a day for forty
days and then forget it."

"Okay, but I don't have to believe it. Right?"

"Right."

I think that Bruce timed it so that the prayer would be finished before the baby was born. I think he understood that that
would be good for the new life about to join us all.

To some degree, it actually worked. I felt better after that fortieth day of gritting my teeth on a daily basis and doing something I truly did not believe in because my friend had asked it of me—for me.

Maybe I was the one who needed healing most of all, and Bruce recognized it. If I had broken my leg, I would have to heal, no matter what had happened to create the broken leg. Bruce knew that and cared enough about me to help set the leg so that it could heal straight and did not remain bent. Part of me knew exactly what was happening. It was that part of me that experienced the love when I died in London, and that part was connected with Bruce, and it knew what he meant when he insisted that I forgive.

The rest of me just could not understand why Robert had engaged in the entire relationship for revenge for something I apparently did when I was just an eighteen-year-old young woman. That is what I could not forgive, and yet I think I truly forgave Robert as Bruce had wanted and understood that it needed to be finished so that the remarkable child who was to be born could enter an atmosphere free of resentment.

The guidance, the first book, the child, those I had learned to love, Barbara, Bruce, Charlotte, and their family had all created the soil, the atmosphere, the love, the nurturing, the light for the growth that meant healing, so that life could do what it must—go on. Forgiveness was the tool for all of that to happen.

Outwardly, it did not appear that it had happened for me since I continued to be intuitively afraid of life without a child's father. Yet inwardly, somewhere within my inner self, something was transformed. For me, that meant, miraculously, that I began slowly to cease being interested in what Robert might think, what he might do, or whether or not he would reappear in my life—ever.

My life within me was finally getting on with itself. However malicious Robert's intentions may have been, life's purpose was the celebration of life itself, and this little baby was well on its way to joining us and bringing whatever its gifts were to all of us who were to love it. The crying diminished. Forgiveness is not easy but happens in the flow of life itself and is a natural process, if you let it. I began to see, thanks to Bruce's persistence and the complete presence of love in my heart, that I was becoming whole again.

Spring, Summer, and Baby

You are the Divine, the child of the living God. That is not
a theory. That is the nature of reality. You are the child of
the living. There is nothing but the living. There is no death.
There is only life and its manifestation.
There is nothing but the Divine.

–The Immortal Now

Spring meant the end of the ski season for Tim. We attended the end-of-the-year awards banquet, and he received a trophy for "most improved." That happens when you are talented and start late at a sport. Tim was also graduating from the eighth grade, and we had to make arrangements. I drove to Idaho Falls, about one hundred miles from Jackson, and bought Tim a nice rust-colored corduroy suit for the ceremonies and the dinner and dance that followed. The graduation was a bursting-at-the-seams-proud mother event and a milestone for Tim. He had a date and a corsage complete with dinner and dance at Teton Village. He was growing up so quickly.

In my custody arrangement with Walter, Tim was to spend a month in the summer with his dad back in the Washington, D.C. area, so at the beginning of June, he took off for Virginia.

Chris came out for two weeks with me, and I was so thrilled to see him that I could hardly take my eyes off him. I was eight months pregnant and not moving quickly. This was only the second time in his entire life that I had been away from my beloved son. He had grown so over the winter. Having been a stay-at-home mom for the first six years of Chris and Tim's young lives and Walt often away on assignment, the boys and I started out close and remained so.

I drove Chris over the Beartooth Highway to see my mother in Red Lodge, Montana. This wildflower-strewn byway is one of the most spectacular drives in the United States. At one point, the drive drops from around ten thousand feet to fifty-five hundred feet in less than sixteen miles. Before the road went in during the 1930s, my mother and Uncle Rodney hiked the sixty-five miles from Red Lodge to Cooke City in the spring to work and then returned in the fall. My mother was an early Montana mountain climber and loved nothing more than losing herself in the backcountry of the Beartooth Mountains for weeks on end. She worked at the Nordquist Ranch, a Montana dude ranch in Sunlight Basin during Ernest Hemingway's time there. She was not overly fond of Hemingway but liked his sixth wife. After the highway was built, my mother used to drive frightened tourists up the pass on their way to Yellowstone at the North Entrance.

Of course, as Chris and I approached the top of Beartooth Pass, he had to, under false pretenses I might add, lure me from the car in order to pellet his unsuspecting mom with freshly made summer snowballs. We had a wonderful time together and a sweet visit with my mother. Chris had not spent a lot of time with this grandmother since Walter and I had lived in the Washington, D.C., area. Mom was back on her feet and spunky.

When I returned to Jackson, I received sad news. My landlord and owner of my log haven in Wilson had decided to use the house himself and gave me thirty days' notice to move. That meant that the move would have to be completed in the last month of my pregnancy. Chris helped with the initial packing but had to return to his dad's. That meant I was facing the entire shaking up of my nest pretty much alone as I was about to go into labor.

I found a cute and very small—and I mean very small—two-bedroom apartment on a stream in downtown Jackson and made arrangements to move in. Of course, I didn't think the baby would come early.

As any gynecologist or husband knows, one of the signs of imminent labor is the extreme nesting that the mother goes through. I was no exception, and with the move to the house on the stream in town, I was busily making preparations for the coming of this baby. I had a crib that I painted and a hand-made "Lambie-Pie" quilt, new clothes—everything. I dreamed of how it would be when I brought my beautiful, new baby home to our new, but small, apartment.

The birth of the baby was still two or three weeks away, or so we thought. Everything was mostly packed, but the living room was still strewn with packing paper, dust, lost keys, and whatever had been under the furniture. The kitchen and bathroom had been packed and moved except for the things I needed to live on, but it was at the stage where everything that didn't fit into boxes was still on the countertops or in the sink. The cleaning still had to be done everywhere, and I was sleeping on Tim's single mattress on the floor of the living room, which made for interesting and very, very pregnant getting up and down. I was tired, alone, and uncomfortable, but I was working with the hope of what it would be like to bring the baby home. Uncomfortable is really not a word for what I was feeling, but I kept telling myself that I just needed to rest.

It was late in evening, and I had worked hard all day and really could not move. I managed to get down on the floor and lie on that mattress hoping just to fall asleep. That didn't work.

I tossed and turned and then needed to get up. Much to my chagrin, I found I simply could not. I was stuck on the floor. I thought of crawling to the phone and calling Barbara for help but could not find the phone and could not crawl.

Then depression, more debilitating than my physical situation, hit me. Here I was, terribly uncomfortable, alone, very tired, and Robert was gone—though he had said that he would be here. I was almost out of money, in the middle of a mess instead of my beautiful dream of a home for my baby, and I could not even get myself off the floor. Then, to make matters worse, the tears began to flow without limit. I just lay there sobbing for at least a half hour, feeling the entire loss of the world I had known and the grief of the last year.

Then I slowly realized that I could be in labor. I knew what labor felt like, and what I was beginning to experience was not just discomfort and depression.

Don't tell me I am in labor on top of everything else? No! I am not going to accept that. I was talking to myself and the Universe at the same time.

I finally realized that if I didn't quit crying and figure out how to get off the floor or at least find the phone, I could have my baby right there in the middle of my predicament.

No, not a good idea.

I pulled myself together, quit crying, figured out a way to roll over, and hitched my hips across the mattress to the divider between the living room and the kitchen. With long legs come long arms. I reached to the top shelf of the divider, used the leverage to turn around to my knees, and hoped it wouldn't break while I pulled and pushed my pregnant, in-labor self up to a standing position. I promptly found the phone, which had disappeared under a pile of clothes, called Barbara, and told her what was happening. My angel, my friend, and my savior came right over and took me to the hospital. In the entire rush, Barbara, who was always organized, did not forget her movie camera, her still camera, her tape recorder, and our friends, Nola and Jerry.

To make a long story short, Barbara was the best Lamaze coach ever, I believe, in the history of birth. In-between labor contractions, Barbara and I decided to do a session. It is one of the funniest tapes we have done since the books began. The first book had been completed in June, but the tape we were doing while I has giving birth was guidance for me. It would go, "Blah, blah, blah," and then you would hear the "Uhhhh, uhhh!" of the contraction, and then go on with what was being said, "Blah, blah, blah." It was saying that we would be starting a second book soon—a second book? I really didn't think that this was a good time to announce that since I was busy giving birth, but I had learned to expect the unexpected from the sessions.

I had my beautiful son around 4:00 A.M. He was so amazing that my heart just flew out somewhere among the stars. At the moment of birth, using the birth without violence, the doctor and nurses put this non-crying new person in a bath of just-right water, his large eyes just looked up happily, and he almost sighed as he saw his mother outside the womb for the first time. They cleaned and wrapped him up and handed him to me. I held him and loved him with everything in my entire being. He embodied my love to the millionth power I had experienced in the accident, and everything else simply vanished.

Robert Returns

You will see that those who seek fear will relinquish that fear in ways you cannot foresee. It is not by the Christian doctrine of repentance. It is through other means within the individual. The individual is all there is and when the fear of earth changes and retribution and anger and lack and all of the fear-based thinking actually comes to a head, then the change is immediate.

–The Immortal Now

My dear friends decided enough was enough. Not wanting to impose on people and having an independent mother, I had not asked for help with the move except for the furniture. Plus, I thought I had time to get it all done.

Nola and Jerry, Barbara and her daughter, Linda, Bruce and Charlotte—I am not exactly sure when or how—managed to complete the move for me, clean up the Wilson house, make my new apartment look adorable for the coming home of the baby, and unpack almost everything except things they thought I might want to put away.

I was thrilled when I came into the apartment and saw their efforts. It looked as if they had had a great time doing it, and they could not have had a more appreciative recipient of their hard work! Upon entry into my family's new home, you were greeted by a small living room made larger by an open dining room and kitchen. The unit looked through large double doors across a green lawn and newly planted trees to a quick stream giggling its way beneath the large hill. Down a short hall to the right was the first bedroom, Tim's room, with a bathroom across the hall, and then the master bedroom was in the back.

The carpeting was rust-colored and matched my Lone Star quilt on the wall. The living room furniture I had made out of four-by-fours was covered with a bright yellow, rust, and white blanket with yellow bolsters. I had gotten a new set of white sheets and a quilt for my bed, and the crib fit nicely in my room. It was clean, fresh, and best of all, still a home. Nola had made a batch of fresh yogurt and other foods and fixed up the refrigerator. Maybe it was because I was nursing, but never in my life have I tasted anything better than that yogurt.

Everyone fell in love with the baby, but Barbara bonded like new glue to that small bundle of soft life. She held him and sang to him and, of course, could not wait to put him into newborn Oshkosh outfits when she changed him. What a pair they made! I could just feel him loving her back as she wrapped him in receiving blankets and cooed to him and told him what a wonder he was.

Robert called while I was in the hospital and said, matter-of-factly, that he would like the baby boy to be named Bradley. He had always liked the name, and Brad was a nice nickname. I told him I would consider it. Robert mostly went by "Bob." I decided to name this beautiful person, Robert Bradley Grabow, with a nickname of "Rob" or, affectionately, "Robbie." Rob Roy had always been a favorite historical character of mine, and I had always liked the name. Done—no one to have to debate with.

My sister, Gretchen, came to visit for a couple of days with her husband, Kip, and daughter, then a teenager. They were climbing the Tetons—again—while they were in Jackson and, as chance would have it, they helped rescue some climbers from a landslide near the Middle Teton.

As with all newborns, I was living baby needs morning, noon, and night—mostly night. Robbie had always been active, but now that he was free of the constraints of the womb, he was having a great time and terribly busy for one so small.

Then when Robbie was about a month old, Robert announced that he was going to fly into Idaho Falls and said I could drive in with the baby and pick him up at the airport. He really did not want to have to rent a car. He said that he would be in Jackson just a day and night and fly out again. I must have been nuts, but I agreed to meet him, so I loaded Robbie in a basket and headed out across the mountain. I do not know if seeing his son registered with Robert, but Robbie was content. Robert had enormous hands so it was very easy for him to rock Robbie to sleep with just one hand.

To say the least, I was nervous having Robert in Jackson. Then Robert did the most unexpected thing. When Robbie was napping, Robert went into the bedroom as he had so many times before. It was as though he thought he was home and nothing had happened in the last year and a half. He closed the door.

Time passed, and I wondered what was going on. He had not come out so I walked into the room, and there Robert lay, completely naked! Expecting something like that was the last thing on my mind—almost like seeing a spiritual corpse. I almost threw up. *Odd response*, I thought to myself, *for a connection that had been an important part in my life. Had I loved this man?* It was one of the most awkward moments I can ever remember. I just turned around and walked back out to the living room. *What on earth was he thinking?* So much for romance!

The visit was short.

SECTION TWO

PASSAGE FROM KARMA

THE SECOND BOOK BEGINS: PASSAGE FROM KARMA

You will see that the present time is much, much more than you can possibly understand using language. That is why the meditation is a necessity when it comes to working with that understanding. It is much, much more than you can even imagine.

—The Immortal Now

I longed for my new son, Robbie, to have a father, but I had to look at my dream of having a nuclear family squarely in the eye. I had to let it go. The myth and the dream had been harsh masters for me. So I was left with the reality of what was happening in my life—not what I wanted it to be. The present, with my children, became the mandate for the process of decision-making.

True to what was said in the session while I was giving birth to Robbie, I learned in a later guidance session with Barbara that it was time for the second book to begin. I thought it should be put off since Robbie was a newborn baby and I was almost out of money. I thought that I should get a job.

Tim came home and had many financial needs. He began his freshman year in high school and joined the football team. He needed special football shoes and more ski equipment for the winter. I was on my feet emotionally enough to substitute teach. I had an Alaska State teaching certificate that had reciprocity with Wyoming so I could make arrangements for a provisional certificate. I also had experience in many other areas since I had financed my bachelor's degree with a combination of blue-collar jobs and student loans. At least, I could find something for part-time income.

The writing, however, was adamant. We had to do *Passage from Karma*, and we had to do it now. It simply said that now was the only time to do the second book, it had to be done, and we did not know why yet. All of Barbara's and my time were needed. End of story. It said that we did not know the future and that there was no choice.

So, arrangements were made for Barbara to meet with me again daily and begin the second book. True to form, the book predicted the number of pages, identified the chapters, and talked about what it would say.

I had to give up nursing Rob because of "milk fever" and a temperature of 104 degrees. Being a redhead and fair-skinned was a problem. Robbie reacted violently to going on formula. After about two weeks, the pediatrician and I realized that Rob was allergic to the lactose in milk, and when we put him on a soy formula, peace returned to the earth or, at least, to our small household.

We would work on the book whenever Robbie was sleeping. Mostly, we did the second book in Barbara's living room with him napping in the warm sun in the window well. He loved that. Rosemary, a former colleague of Barbara's who had recently moved in with her, would disappear when we worked, which I appreciated since I always experienced a slight uneasiness around her. We would end the session when Robbie started to stir. The writing said that, in a larger sense, he was trying to be cooperative with what was happening and was aware of what was being done, but that he was getting hungry.

Barbara's roommate transcribed the sessions almost as soon as they were recorded. By the time we had finished our sessions for the second book, the book tapes had been transcribed.

Passage from Karma used the analogy of humanity being like a chick inside an egg, as it had in *Passage from Fear*. It called that world inside the egg the World of Fear paradigm. To the chick, the existence inside the egg was all there was since the chick was not yet aware of anything beyond the egg. I compared that to my previous belief that there was life, then death, then heaven. It was not until I died that I saw beyond that world—much like the chick— and experienced that there was simply life and love in the present moment. I existed, egg or no egg, death or no death. The being that existed within my world of the egg expanded to the understanding that the presence of the joy I was beginning to feel more and more was all that exists.

So the chick believes, and reinforces that belief with all of the evidence surrounding it, that what exists is life within the egg. The chick could not be convinced otherwise since that is all that its physical senses allow.

Then *Passage from Karma* went on to use the analogy of the egg tooth. The egg tooth is a sharp projection that grows out of the chick's beak at the right time and allows the chick to peck at the egg from the inside and break the shell, releasing itself to the world outside the confines the egg.

It then said the books that I and others were doing, along with global prayer and meditation, were providing humanity with that egg-tooth for breaking out of the egg to discover the entire world that exists beyond the World of Fear.

Passage from Karma went further with the analogy and said that when the chick breaks from the egg, it has no desire to return to the confines of the egg. Coming out of the egg is so natural to the chick that the expansion of its world is hardly noticed. Good point.

It also said that the scientific community was frequently leading, to some degree, over the theological community because the churches had relinquished so much of their true spiritual power in order to control others. All of this was occurring while quantum physics was expanding further as a concept.

A WORLD CHANGING

Life itself is church, religion, truth, all of the things that have been categorized into the realm of what is called theology but, in fact, is so much more universal that it is impossible to confine it to those areas of thought. It becomes more and more contrived, the more the individual attempts to limit the understanding of the nature of God.

–*The Immortal Now*

Like the analogy of the chick, my world was changing. I was not crying five hours a day and was enjoying my sons enormously. I could feel the beauty of the Tetons coming in through all of my newly awakening senses as the aspen began to change into their glimmering gold-coin fall plumage in stark contrast to the evergreen. Everything seemed alive and almost new to me.

After Robert's last visit, he had nearly disappeared from my thoughts. He may have sensed my losing interest in him as he began calling frequently at the most inappropriate times. I learned later that this is common with sexual predators.

High school was going full bore for Tim, and he loved it. He quit the football team, and the students protested by ignoring him when he would come into the lunchroom. Tim knew that skiing was his first love, and he didn't want injury to slow down what was looking like a year where he would break through as a national, world-class skier. Tim stuck by his guns. As a freshman, he was growing like a weed and becoming the kind of man that girls giggled about and loved to talk to. He was busy.

Chris was still with his dad and attending St. Stephen's in Washington, D.C. He was also on a roll with strong academic credentials for getting into an Ivy League college, which was his dream.

The only fear that still truly gripped me was that of lack. I was running out of money fast. Tim had taken a part-time job at the Stagecoach Inn to cover many of his expenses. I just could not make ends meet. I began to sell everything that was extra just to keep the second book going. One of the things I felt most guilty about was that I sold my diamond ring from my marriage to David. It had belonged to his grandmother. Aargh! I sold a three-hundred-dollar double down sleeping bag for fifty dollars and have always regretted that, but food was getting short. I told Barbara not to tell Bruce and Charlotte what was happening financially and that I would work it out. I refused to take any loans from Barbara, not that she had money to spare.

Barbara was also experiencing a fear of her own. The hiatal hernia that had almost killed her before I came along was acting up again. She was taking drugs to suppress the pain, and I would go to the local pharmacy to pick up her prescriptions. Having been raised largely as an ecumenical Christian Scientist, I had no idea what Percodan was and why the pharmacist was so picky about everything.

The threat of another surgery began to emerge like a callus created by ill-fitting tennis shoes. Barbara was in a dilemma. Before her last surgery, she had been estranged from her son that she loved dearly and thought she had nothing to live for. She had accepted the possibility that she probably would not survive. That surgery had almost killed her. Then, Robbie and I came along. She adored us. This time she wanted to live, and she was torn about having the surgery. Barbara and I had numerous discussions about this, and I was her sounding board.

Barbara's roommate, Rosemary, promoted the idea of surgery whenever she could. She was also very anxious for Barbara to have any painkillers she might want. Then she became adamant about Barbara changing her will. As we were finishing the second book, she persuaded Barbara to leave her beautiful, paid-for condominium at Teton Village to her in her will, cutting out Barbara's son entirely. I did not find out about this until later.

I could never figure out how Barbara's roommate pulled that off. Ostensibly supportive of the work we were doing, Rosemary transcribed and typed, ironically, *Passage from Fear* as we were recording *Passage from Karma*. I was caring for a teenager, worried about money, had a newborn, beautiful baby, and was dictating *Passage from Karma*. What was happening with Barbara's roommate was simply flying under the radar.

At one point, Bruce and Charlotte took me aside and warned me about trying to complete the second book too fast because of what happened to Edgar Cayce. Bruce and Charlotte were close friends of Hugh Lynn Cayce, Edgar Cayce's son, and Charlotte said that Cayce should have been limited to a maximum of twenty minutes a day of channeling in order to stay healthy. As Cayce's fame grew, desperate people would seek him, and he would acquiesce to much more than the twenty minutes. "What was he supposed to do, turn a child away?" Charlotte said.

Both Bruce and Charlotte attributed Cayce's early demise to a kind of psychic exhaustion. We weren't anything like Cayce, but we were getting exhausted. The writing kept insisting that *Passage from Karma* had to be finished though, so we were

obedient. The writing had always been so uncannily accurate.
Little did we know what lay ahead.

ALASKA AND SOUL MATES

You will see that the truth is much, much more than
you even see. It is like a straight line. It is like a prairie
without a sky. It is a simple thing. It is not intricate and not
complicated. You will understand
the nature of timeless truth.

–*The Immortal Now*

We finished *Passage from Karma* in early November. Then my money simply ran out. I ran out of things to sell and was desperate and really did not want to let Bruce and Charlotte know what was happening. They were so kind and generous, but I thought that talking with them about my financial situation was the equivalent of asking for money. I valued them and their friendship too much. Pride or whatever prevailed. For the first time since the writing began, I ignored the advice given. The writing kept assuring me that there would be supply.

By chance, I called my friend Rosie Porter in Bethel, Alaska. I had met Rosie about four years earlier when I taught the Fox-fire-type program for the Lower Kuskokwim School District and stayed at her place, Leen's Lodge, with other boarders and her family. We became fast friends.

One night while we were visiting, the topic of premonitions came up. I risked and told Rosie that I had premonitions as a child and that I knew early one morning that my healthy-looking father was going to die later that day of a heart attack.

"Of course," Rosie replied, much to my surprise.

I let out a sigh and smiled. Here was someone for whom my world was natural.

"I have angels," she said. "Sometimes when things are stressful, I go lie down, and literally before my head hits the pillow, I am taken up and comforted. They are there."

We were two people who, though different, had simply been woven of the same fabric and knew it from the start.

Rosie was one of the most powerful women in bush (rural interior) Alaska at the time. She started *The Tundra Drums,* which became the largest weekly newspaper in the state and had been on television in Anchorage and Fairbanks as a weather person and news reporter. She owned her own ad agency, was on many boards in the state, and interviewed gubernatorial candidates at any given election.

A beautiful tall blonde and intellectual force, Rosie was probably the single most truthful person I had ever known. She and her siblings basically raised themselves as children in Jersey City, New Jersey, and her independence was palpable. If you wanted verifiable answers to questions, you asked Rosie. She could judge both ends of a bull and knew what came out of the south end when it was north-facing. I never saw her once mince words.

When Rosie was in a pinch, she would ask me to write stories for the *Tundra Drums.* I quickly learned that she wrote that forty-eight-page weekly newspaper with an exceedingly sharp stiletto. Yet, she had a great sense of fun. There was nothing better than sitting down with her staff and writing hysterically funny headlines, many of which were used by Jay Leno in his "Time for Headlines" segment on *The Tonight Show.* One I remember was the caption for a story in which a man was arrested for stealing a sausage from Swanson's grocery store in Bethel. It read, "Man Arrested for Salami Concealment."

When I talked with Rosie on the phone, I discussed my financial situation with her. She said that she could not afford to send money but needed a part-time reporter for the newspaper and would pay me twelve-hundred dollars a month. She said I could stay as short a time as I needed, and she would send the plane ticket for me.

I will never understand my thought process at the time. I had been told by the writing that I would be provided for, and it had never been wrong. I did understand that Tim could not leave school while I went to Alaska to provide for our needs. I had comfort in the presence of Rosie and knew she would be true to her word. My reasoning went something like this: A+B+X=Z. Nothing made sense.

I decided to find a babysitter for Tim and my beloved baby, Robbie, and take off for Alaska to make enough money to pay for the next month's rent. How could I have ever thought I could leave that baby? Perhaps I had some odd gene that creates a lack of oxygen to the brain during times of extreme stress and financial lack, thus creating the fertile ground for exceptionally poor decisions. I do not have a better explanation.

I found a very good babysitter for Robbie, left Tim, and flew to Alaska. I cannot even describe how my heart felt at leaving my baby and Tim. I threw up the entire trip on the plane, and I wasn't sick. The writing said that the supply would be there, but where was it? Mostly I had lost faith in myself and still found it unnatural to rely on the Universe for whatever was needed. After the undeniable proofs and gifts I had been given since the accident, I should have known it was within the present, within the being of the individual, and not in my planning, but I just could not see it with my old awareness. Love, however, had more in store for me.

I flew from Idaho Falls to Anchorage, waited out a brief stopover, and headed out to bush Alaska. Rosie met me at the small Bethel airport.

Bethel is two things in November: flat and white. I was in a village of about fifteen hundred people, largely Alaska Native, on the flattest part of the flat tundra huddled against the mighty, frozen Kuskokwim River in the middle of southwestern Alaska. It is 450 air miles to the nearest road other than the fifteen-mile Bethel "highway." Cars were clunkers, worked and reworked. The only time new or used vehicles could be brought in by barge from Seattle was during the summer when the river thawed.

Houses were mostly single, small, almost makeshift huts built on stilts instead of on the tundra, which consists of permafrost. Permafrost is permanently frozen ground until you build a house on it and heat it. Unfortunately, many a house had sunk slowly into unknown places. These tiny homes were scattered around the large, yellow submarine-like hospital and various flat, rectangular federal buildings painted in that all-too-familiar beige with a hint of pink. Bethel was famous for its one tree that was celebrated with a two-sided sign, one side of which read, "Welcome to Bethel National Forest." The other side of the sign read, "You are now leaving the Bethel National Forest."

Winter comes in mid-October and does not leave until late-May, and winter had arrived with a vengeance. It was not uncommon in Bethel for whiteouts with raging winds of seventy miles an hour and minus seventy degrees. Even in the most bleak of storms, there is a colorful interplay of the light of the area and the ground it permeates. Sunsets are often a hot pink darkening to a mauve and can occur mid-afternoon in the winter.

The light in November was dim and beautiful in its somber tones. It is almost as though light feels that its energy is frozen and limited. But in spite of that, I believe it is an understatement to say that Bethel is beautiful. There is no place in Bethel that nature does not sweep constantly with her broom like a compulsive housewife wanting to compensate for a modest dwelling place. The ground is always taking on new forms. Car tracks disappear almost instantly, and their ridges morph into small, stark, clean bumps in the road. Drifts cozy up to brown tarpaper walls and the red-and-white grocery store, forming cones around street signs along the way. Everywhere the wind rearranges its house. Even D-9 Cats become covered halfway with blankets around their spiked tracks. The cross at the top of the Moravian church stands defiantly against the weather's brush of energy and remains a beacon of the West's intrusion into the furthest reaches of the earth.

Rosie, her family, and the *Tundra Drums* were still at Leen's Lodge but were planning a new building with a fourteen-room bed and breakfast on the top floor and a state-of-the-art newspaper office complete with a row of computers on the main floor. Leen's Lodge, which had been built on the tundra by westerners who did not understand permafrost, was sinking into the ground by several inches a year!

With its ancient peeling white paint, the lodge had at least eight bedrooms on the top floor. A living room, a kitchen with a roaring stove and commercial sinks, and a dining room were on the bottom floor. Rosie was one of the best cooks I had ever known and often had at least fifteen hungry people who just decided to stop by for dinner.

I arrived a day before Thanksgiving, Rosie's favorite holiday. I shook off at the front door. Rosie's two children, Kendall and Gregory, then teenagers, were in front of the TV in the same position on the couch just as they were three years ago. Even though my life had completely changed, my arrival was like that of the postman. They acknowledged me, but were obviously involved in their program.

Rosie was glad to have me back and showed me to my room. We had kept up with periodic phone calls. I was comforted to see her, yet my heart was heavy, and I was at a loss in spite of Rosie's graciousness and friendship. I called Tim and the babysitter to make sure everything was okay at home and set about to help in the kitchen.

Things were in a flurry. Rosie was expecting at least thirty people for Thanksgiving and was making preparations for multiple everything—turkeys, side dishes, desserts, drinks, hors d'oeuvres—cooked with panache, international sauces, and largess. I went right to work wondering what really was happening for all of us. Why was I here? I belonged with my family. I loved Rosie and those around me, but I was part of my baby and could not bear to think that I was away from him. I ached to have him in my arms. I tried to be grateful, but I knew what was happening for me just was not right. I visited with Rosie about it, and she understood as she always did. She was truly what the books called a soul mate—and always had been.

Rosie and I got up early the next morning, Thanksgiving Day, and were busy organizing and doing whatever had to be done. The phone rang about ten o'clock in the morning. Rosie answered. She spoke with whoever was on the line and began to beam. I was wondering who could bring so much joy to my friend's face. She beckoned for me to come over and said that the call was for me.

"You are not going to believe this, Pat. Charlotte McArthur is on the phone."

I was stunned.

"Charlotte and Bruce ran into Barbara McCormick, and they asked how you were doing. Barbara told them. Charlotte said they had come into some money unexpectedly and want to give it to you to come back to Jackson! Patricia, you can go home! Here, speak to Charlotte."

Rosie handed me the phone. I was shaking in disbelief.

"It's true," Charlotte said calmly, as always. "Bruce and I are concerned that you didn't tell us what you were going through. Please come home as soon as you can. We did get money unexpectedly. I asked Bruce, and we wondered why we got that. Then we ran into Barbara the next day. We both knew instantly what we needed to do."

I broke down and just cried.

Charlotte interrupted me, "I didn't call to make you cry, Patricia."

"No, Charlotte, it is so good to hear your voice, and I can't stand to be away."

Rosie was saying in the background, "Pat, listen to Charlotte!"

"Yes, I'm trying."

Charlotte continued, "Pat, why didn't you tell us?"

"I'm sorry, Charlotte. I just did not know what else to do, and I didn't want to impose on anyone."

"That is nonsense, Patricia, dear."

I could not believe what I was hearing, and Rosie was giggling.

I could go back to Jackson! I don't remember exactly what I said to Charlotte, but I remember more gratitude than I could put in words.

It was the worst and best Thanksgiving of my life!

I was on the next plane out of Bethel, and after getting to my apartment and paying the babysitter, I lost myself in my beautiful sons. Tim had a lot to tell me, and contentment was in Rob's eyes. I called Chris, too, and caught up on the latest events in his life. My heart was full.

The writing had said that the supply would be there, and it was! I vowed that I would pay Bruce and Charlotte back and eventually did.

New Challenges

When one loses a friend to what is called death, one does not lose a friend. The individual consciousness loses a conscious creation of who that friend actually was, but the individual simply remains.

–The Immortal Now

Of course, Barbara was thrilled to have me back, and I thanked her for letting Bruce and Charlotte know that I had gone to Alaska. Things had changed much for Barbara in the short time I had been gone. The pain she experienced had increased. Rosemary, her roommate, convinced her to go under the knife again as a remedy—even though the last surgery had not been helpful and it had nearly killed her.

Barbara was not unhealthy, but the extreme invasiveness of the procedure would jeopardize anyone's life, not to mention someone in her mid-sixties. She had described the surgery to me in detail during our long conversations, and I could not believe she was even considering having it again and said so.

We asked for guidance, but this time, the writing did not give it. Rosemary persisted in saying how the surgery would fix everything. I replied that it hadn't before, so why would it now a year later? Even the doctor was reticent about proceeding. Barbara was simply tired of the pain, and Rosemary's insistence won the day.

The surgery was scheduled to be performed at the Jackson Hospital. I was in a cold sweat, similar to the one I had experienced when I was ten years old and knew that my father was going to die. I arranged for a babysitter for Robbie and told myself that it was going to be okay, trying to silence my greater sense of things. Tim insisted on being at the hospital with Barbara as much as he could. He was very fond of her, as was anyone who truly knew her.

The surgery was performed, and I could tell as soon as it was over and Barbara began to wake up that something was not right. Apparently, the surgeon had not properly sutured the wound, and any liquids that Barbara took in after the surgery went into her intestinal cavity. Worried, though I tried not to show it, I would not leave Barbara's side. Late that evening, we were in her room. Her bed was on one side, and at the entrance was a curtain pulled slightly back from the wall. I was looking at her, and suddenly, she looked up beyond me where the curtain was pulled back, and her face just glowed.

Not taking her eyes off her vision, she said, "Pat do you see him—the man over by the curtain? Do you see that fabric? Did you see his robes? I have never seen anything so beautiful! Have you ever seen anything like that?"

I turned to look, and told her I couldn't see it, and listened while she, in a state of pure joy, described what she saw. That was the last time she was conscious. I spent the night by her bed telling myself that she was just sleeping. I knew better. She died of peritonitis the next morning. Gratefully, Barbara's last conscious act was at least witnessing something beyond the mundane and surrounded with the returned love of a friend.

When I watched her flatline after hours of being unconscious, I was in a state of complete shock. My heart was racing. When the doctor said she was gone, I cried, "No!" There was no consoling me as I walked out of the hospital sobbing and then returned to be with her body. She was the purest friend I had ever known in my life. She, along with the handful of what the writings called soul mates, had brought me salvation—Bruce, Charlotte, David, my children, including my new baby, and my friend Rosie Porter. It was not a theological, hypothetical salvation. The people to whom I had been led had literally saved me.

But I could not save Barbara. Why? Why could I not do for her what she had done for me? I was wretched.

I finally came to and began to think of what Barbara would want me to do. Even though Barbara did not request it, I decided to let her son know that he had lost his mother. I called Rosemary to get his number and could not believe what I heard.

"You'll spoil everything," she said.

"What? How would I spoil everything by letting Barbara's son know that his mother just died?"

What was this woman doing? Then I remembered that she got Barbara to change her will, leaving to her and not to her child—her condo, her furniture, her library, and her car. I hung up and called Linda, Barbara's adopted daughter, got the number, and spoke to a shocked, loving child of my wonderful friend. That night, Nola Kathleen, a seer in her own way, had a dream that Barbara came to her and said that her roommate had killed her.

We made arrangements for a memorial service. We were trying so hard to move forward in the stream of life, but like a log stuck at a bridge, it was impossible to move. The more the stream pushed against me, the more I wedged in. Linda made arrangements with Rosemary to scatter Barbara's ashes in the Snake River. I just could not go after what had happened with Barbara's son. I had my own service and spent time with Nola.

The loss was overwhelming. When was it going to stop? I couldn't move.

Weeks later, Chris came out for Christmas, and Chris, Tim, Robbie, and I had a wonderful time together as a family. Chris and Tim skied endlessly during that time, but there was an essential member of our spiritual family missing: Barbara.

ANOTHER LIFE AND THE SOURCE

This is only one plane of existence. You are functioning on literally thousands of planes of existence in any given second. The reason for the books coming into being is so that you will expand consciously as well as unconsciously and be aware of the nature of the Presence of God, of your own unlimited nature within.

–The Immortal Now

I was lost for a month after Barbara's passing, though I kept things going. I had come to rely on her friendship in so many ways—her support, her smile, and her adoration of Robbie—everything.

Bruce and Charlotte sold their home in Jackson and bought a beautiful place they named Trinity Ranch just outside of Darby, Montana. They built houses for themselves and their son, Thomas, and his family. I was in touch with them regarding Barbara, and with guidance Bruce, Charlotte, and I did a session in which we were told to edit the first book at their ranch.

I packed up my little Toyota truck with my then six-month-old child and drove to Darby to work with Bruce and Charlotte for two weeks. Tim was off to another national ski race with the team and his coach, Fred, at Snow Basin in Utah.

Bruce and Charlotte rented a motel room in Darby and made arrangements for meals at the adjoining restaurant. Robbie and I snuggled right into our temporary home.

Bruce was still busily writing his book on the Universal Laws based on the Cayce readings. He had nearly a roomful of boxes filled with his research and was struggling to find the way to communicate the essence of that work. He was also doing taxes for the ranch and their enterprises, so it was an effort for Bruce and Charlotte to follow the guidance given to help me, although they would never say it. They simply said yes when the writing suggested it, no questions asked.

I drove from the motel to the turnoff for Trinity Ranch. It was out of Shangri-La. The entrance to the ranch crossed a beautiful stream, passed the ranch manager's house, climbed a hill into the tall Ponderosa pine trees, and revealed at either end of a meadow the two houses Bruce and Charlotte had built. Their son's house was to the right, a stunningly beautiful, hefty log structure with a fireplace in the center. To the left of the meadow was the octagonal, white dream house Bruce and Charlotte had created. I parked the car and entered the living room from the second floor. The basement was devoted to a study and a growing area for hydroponic plants.

We hugged and spent some time visiting—just good friends catching up on everything. Robbie fell instantly in love with Bruce and Charlotte with all of his little baby heart.

"How is Tim doing?" Charlotte loved and admired him for his presence throughout everything that had transpired over the last year.

"He's with his coach at Snow Basin as we speak."

"Wonderful!"

Robbie laughed and giggled. Bruce and Charlotte had a little walker to entertain him while we did our sessions. Since their granddaughter Elisha was two weeks younger than Robbie, they had all of the appropriate toys in the house for him. He was in baby heaven, and I had come home—again.

We went through the chapters of the first book with a session for each. I would "use the light" and go into a meditative state, and either Bruce or Charlotte would ask for guidance and run the tape recorder. Generally, we would discuss what we wanted to know before we began. All of the sessions were recorded on tape.

It was fascinating to all of us that when I was in the meditative state Robbie was either napping or surprisingly quiet, as if he was also meditating, just as he had done in utero.

One day, we decided to do a session on the Source of the material for the books. We thought it would take about twenty minutes or so and decided to do it during Robbie's nap. Then we had other plans for the day.

Bruce had compiled a list of questions he had about the Source of the material ahead of time.

We began, and the Source said that it was a good thing to have the session with Bruce and Charlotte since I had a tendency to ask the writing the same question over and over: "Am I not just talking to myself?" at which point the writing would reply,

No, but you should talk to yourself more often. You are a very interesting person.

Bruce and Charlotte chuckled quietly. It was true.

Or, I would often ask, "Isn't this just my subconscious speaking?"

The writing would say,

No, there is only consciousness on this plane of existence. You are functioning on literally thousands of planes of existence in any given second.

Okay, so much for my simple approach!

Then Bruce became serious, knowing that this was an opportunity that might not come again. He began asking questions from his list and jumped right in with the most direct ones.

Here are the words of this encounter from the actual transcript of the tape of the session, complete with Bruce's background chuckle and Charlotte's occasional quip.

Bruce: "I am trying to understand from where the Source of the material for the books is originating."

It simply replied, "*Yes.*"

Bruce: "The first question is: are you the Ultimate Source of All, and is there no greater awareness than you? Or are you a portion of that with equal awareness."

The Source replied through me,

> *Yes. It is a difficult question to answer. The book on karmic debt will clarify some of the question.*

[With Barbara's death, the transcription of *Passage from Karma* had not been completed.]

The Session went on:

> *The language is very difficult to deal with. In your language, you have assumed that partial is separate from a partial adjacent to it, when it is actually all a flowing whole, such as individuals are a flowing whole, and that a partial awareness is intermeshed with the other "partial awareness," like salt in the stew is not separate from the stew.*

> *You will see that awareness is awareness like love is love. When it is felt, it is a universal truth. One does not experience a different grade of love from another; when they love, they share the same reality. The events surrounding that reality are different, but the reality is the same and not measurable. That is, you cannot measure love by*

saying, "I love three liters or five liters of love." You love. It
is a separate state of consciousness from, for example, the
state of consciousness you went through when working
on your income tax, my son.

Bruce and Charlotte let out a snicker. Bruce had been struggling with his taxes in the downstairs for several days. It was the first year that they had to do taxes for a ranch, and the learning curve was steep.

But to continue with the understanding of the Source:

The Source is not Patricia, in any way. She is only a chan-
nel for that. She was chosen because her motives were
truly pure, and she truly would not abuse it in any way.
She has had many opportunities in her lifetime to abuse
power and has never chosen to do so. Because of that, she
became a channel for a separate state of consciousness
from a World of Fear.

The Source, throughout the book, is from what is termed
the "Spiritual Universe." It is like a ray of sunlight that is
energy and is not limited to the interaction on the plant
that is produced in photosynthesis. But the photosynthe-
sis is the effect, and so the Source is Universal Light. The
photosynthesis that is occurring is the book itself, and the
communication is from that Source.

Light has its own character and is universal. So you
could say that the Source is Universal Light. That does
not answer your question. If you wish to go back to spe-
cifics of your question, you may.

Bruce was encouraged so he went back to part of his original question with a different tact. "This Universal Light, which is the Source, could be termed the Ultimate Source?"
The Source came back surprisingly to Bruce. It said,

> *Yes, it could be termed the Ultimate Source, but it is not. There is no Ultimate Source. There is an interplay, even within the earth of life, but each life has its own expression. In this case, you are dealing with the expression of that Light. The tree will express that Light in a separate way from a verbal expression; in this particular case, it is needed for Homo sapiens and verbal communication and on this plane. It is the clearest that can be expressed, given the limitations surrounding you.*
>
> *You must understand that this is just one plane of existence, and Love is a hint of the nature of God. But this is not the totality of God. You are exploring, at this point, the broad sense of God, which is a hint similar to the rock and the mountain. The rock is not the mountain, but it has characteristics of the mountain and is certainly worthy of looking at to study what could conceivably be a mountain. Looking at the rock, you cannot envision the size, shape, depth, breadth, and life support system that a mountain truly is. However, it is a very broad attempt to understand the breadth with which you are dealing. Infinity is characteristic of God but not understandable at this time on this plane.*

It looked like that was it, so Bruce said, "Through this material, are we tapping an aspect of infinity?"
The Source replied,

Yes, you are, and within your Larger Being, you under-stand that, as those who are ready will understand that as well. This is frightening to Patricia. She can face this as well.

It was true. It was frightening to me.

Bruce went on to ask if this Source was the same source as for Edgar Cayce, and it replied, "*Yes,*" but from a different per-spective. Then Bruce asked if it were the same source as a book that Bruce and Charlotte had heard of, *A Course in Miracles,* and it replied, "*Yes.*"

Charlotte had been working on a book on the Essenes and asked if the Source was the same source for that also, and it replied, "*Yes.*" That was to take a remarkable twist later, though we did not know about it at the time.

Bruce asked how to address the Source. It replied,

You cannot. You cannot name feelings; this is very impor-tant that you not find a name.

It not only said that that would place a limitation but went on to add,

It would also, for those who are living in a World of Fear, allow them to harm those who are continuing this very important work. It is important that there be protection for those who are working on this. It is critical. Cayce used terms that he knew would allow people to slough off the Source comfortably and yet listen to the work. It is important to do the same.

Bruce discussed his friend Al Miner in Florida, who used the source he called "Lama Sing" and asked for a comparison. The Source said an interesting thing.

The term "Spiritual Universe" has been frequently used in the automatic writing. The term that has also been used within a larger sense is "soul mate." It is similar to what Lama Sing is using. It is, however limiting itself by limiting its source. And that is functional, because if the source is limited when one is dealing with a limited reality and fearful, then it is more acceptable to those who listen; you cannot communicate until you are able to communicate with individuals where they are.

Later, I wondered if that related to me at that point in my growth. I had so much to absorb, and it was compassionate. It said that Bruce could effectively stop the session and reformulate the question if he wished.

The Source said that it was important, at this time, to supersede personality.

Undaunted, Bruce moved ahead with his next prepared question. "It is You of whom Christ spoke when He said that we should love God with all our heart, body, mind, and soul and love our neighbors as ourselves?"

The Source replied, "*It is not I.*" It had always insisted that everything exists within the individual and that there was no exterior reality. It remained true to the message.

It is within the individual. There is a difficult communication that must take place in this area. It is the Christ within that is to be loved. When the Christ within, as Jesus understood, is loved, there is a direct link with what has been traditionally called God. Then the individual understands all that he or she needs to understand and naturally loves what has been traditionally called God. It is not possible to do so without the use of the White Light at this point, loving the Christ within the individual and not loving a defined sense of God, but more discovering what exists once that link is established.

The idea of loving God, as the Biblical admonition gives, is loving a preconception of God. Like a child learning to walk, the child truly does not understand what walking is at the point that he or she learns to walk. But the child finds delight in the process. When you love the Christ within you—it cannot be emphasized enough that the Christ exists within all life—then you go through the process of learning to walk not knowing where the walking process is leading you. You will discover more and more aspects of My Being, my son.

This is, again, difficult to answer because few words in this language express the feeling experienced when this occurs. It is not that you should love God. It is that you cannot help doing it. Like a plant processing sunlight, it is not that the plant should process sunlight. It is the life of the plant. And I am your life.

Bruce said, "Thank you. That is very helpful," to which the Source said simply, "*Yes.*"

Then it went on offering to allow further clarification of terms and said that it was important that questions continue regarding the Source and implied that Bruce and Charlotte might be the ones to do that since,

Patricia is frightened by it and asks the same questions frequently related to her fear.

I had been so beautifully guided for this work. No one but Bruce and Charlotte McArthur, who had been so very loving and open to the Cayce works as they were, could have been able to do the session on the Source and keep going. I would have been unable even to ask the questions to bring out necessary answers.

Bruce went on: "As I understand it, in another analogy, Spiritual Universe might represent, in such terms, a huge reservoir of water that various individuals can tap through a pipe leading to that reservoir. Patricia represents this pipe, and others such as Al Miner [Lama Sing] do too; so the knowledge becomes available to those who are seeking, to the degree that they can comprehend within their language and dimensional understanding."

The response was interesting.

Yes, to the degree that they can overcome what they have been taught from an introduction into a World of Fear. In time, the pipe will not be needed at all, and the reservoir will be tapped by everyone. And that is the goal, that the individual understands.

Bruce then asked the question dearest to his heart, "Would the transition from the World of Fear to the World of Love be the equivalent of the individual becoming Christ?"

Unlike other questions, essentially, the Source did not answer. It said that it is not easy to understand and would be clear in possibly another work. It said Barbara was present supporting Patricia metaphysically, and please ask the next question.

Bruce asked why the World of Fear was necessary in the first place.

It is not now. It was a survival system that allowed for an evolution that had its day. It is a difficult concept but can be translated into the term, "definition by antithesis;" that is, understanding what is by its opposite. With the knowledge of what is, there was always a light in the room of darkness, like a crack in the door or a seam in a wall or whatever. There is not absolute darkness anywhere, my son.

The Source spoke of Bruce and Charlotte's adjustment to the work coming through me and assured them that I would be helpful. Bruce spoke of the book discouraging study groups. The Source said that it was not a directive but:

It is a general feeling that when groups are formed a social group begins, and one who explores receives ideas from others. In the present time, you are not interacting with social groups. You are with Me. In fact, social groups occur essentially in the past, as does language. This is difficult to understand. From the third book to be written, you will better understand the necessity for not having groups. But, you can do whatever you choose, for you are always being led.

As a final question, Bruce asked if Barbara were here. She was on all of our minds constantly as we all grieved our loss. The Source implied that Barbara was with us and then said that she would visit me when she needed help to cope with her own transition and would love me through this period into a period of great joy. It said that she had graduated but could always return to the classroom like a guest lecturer and could now be of more help than she could have been before. It said that we would understand even better the soul mate concept when the third book was written.

Then, the amazing session on the Source was finished, and I gradually came to.

Bruce, Charlotte, and I were transfixed and could not move—literally were unable to move our bodies at all. We were stuck in our seats completely drained of any energy we had earlier when we had planned how the day would go. Rob was asleep. The dog was even wiped out on the front steps.

Bruce chuckled, "Well, Patricia, you're a pipe."

I smiled. As usual, I heard much of the session, but not all. During a session, what was being said sounded at a distance, and at times I would be so far "out there" that I could not, and really was not, interested in what was being said, much like when I died—more so with this session than with others.

We spoke softly of what was said during the session but still could not move. Charlotte was the first to make the actual observation. She commented that she probably had never been as drained of energy as she was at this moment. Bruce and I piped up that we were in her camp so we just hung out waiting for some semblance of anything to return. Eventually, Rob stirred, and Charlotte got us all a cup of tea, but the rest of the day was simply shot. Nada.

In a later session, the Source said that ideas actually have energy and that the power of the ideas expressed essentially took all we had. True.

WE FINISH EDITING AND
HAVE DECISIONS TO MAKE

*All of life is in a state of transformation, of prayer, of awe at
this time. There is no satisfaction outside of the self within.*

−*The Immortal Now*

I stayed at Trinity Ranch for a couple of days after we completed the editing of the first book. It was a lengthy process but fascinating. We went through the first book, chapter by chapter, asking through the channeling process for any corrections and clarifications. Everything was recorded on tape.

Then Tim called and was very ill with exacerbated flu-like symptoms. In addition, he had fallen at a major race at Snow Basin, and we needed to find out what was causing the excruciating pain in his knees. His coach suspected Osgood-Schlatter disease, a condition common in young athletes where the quadriceps, the large muscles at the front top of the leg, pull the patellar tendon away from the still-soft, developing area of the shin bone just below the knee. It is extremely painful, and Tim was ripe for it since he was a boy, growing around a foot between the eighth and ninth grades, and a skier with highly developed quads literally pulling at that growth plate. One of Bruce and Charlotte's neighbors in Jackson was making the three-hundred-mile trip to her ranch in Darby and was willing to bring Tim over. Tim arrived that day, much to our relief.

Charlotte was a master's degree-level nurse and loved Tim dearly so she went right to work checking him out and making him comfortable. We found that the first treatment was RICE:

rest, ice, compress, and elevate. We could not return to Jackson until Tim was doing better, so we stayed with our wonderful hosts. We were family, the McArthurs and my little family, and the healing taking place everywhere was obvious. Charlotte acted exactly like Tim's mother. She had many of the Edgar Cayce remedies as well as traditional medicine, and she used everything in her repertoire.

Bruce asked me what I might do when we were finished with the editing. Had I given it some thought?

I had thought about nothing else. What to do? What I really wanted to do was return to Alaska and earn a living. I also needed some closure with Robert.

I told Bruce that I was thinking of going back to Alaska, and he looked at me as if to say, "Are you nuts?"

"Did the writing give you any guidance?"

"No, Bruce, nothing. Sometimes it does that, as it did with Barbara, when the decision is one in which it is best that the guidance comes from within. I don't know; it just seems that I am not over whatever I was supposed to learn."

Bruce chucked, as he often did, and said, "Or, you are just a bit stubborn."

"Possibly. I agree it seems stupid."

Silence was all that came out of my friend. He spoke without speaking.

I had even thought of asking Robert to arrange a short stint on the North Slope for me just to get back on my feet financially since most of my traditional employment was long-term and had a protocol to it—particularly teaching. I had money left over from what Bruce and Charlotte had given me and could get by, but for how long without work? I applied in Jackson for teaching positions, and there were none, and they paid almost nothing. I could have substituted, but it was sketchy and not enough to support my family. I had tried waitressing at the Stage Coach Inn but could hardly make babysitting costs with the money, and it did not even occur to me to seek child support from Robert.

Before I left Bruce and Charlotte's, I had a dream of Robert coming into the kitchen, wearing a beautiful turquoise shirt, and being genuinely loving. Bruce and Charlotte said that the kitchen, according to Cayce (who explained dreams as symbology), was service to humanity and the turquoise was spirituality. Interesting. It seemed hopeful. But finally, Bruce, in a completely uncharacteristic way, simply said it seemed to him that my going back to the North Slope was not a good idea. It took a lot for him to say that because he interfered in almost no one's life. He just offered support. Charlotte agreed with her husband, although it was uncharacteristic of her to interfere in a situation like this.

I Return to Alaska

The world of love is within the present, is always here, is within the heart, is within the being of each individual. It is not separate from the being.

–The Immortal Now

The writing said it was okay to contact Robert! It took all the courage I had to call him. I told him I needed a job for my family and that I understood that our relationship was over.

He said he would see what he could do. I went back to Jackson and packed. Then I received a call from Robert who said he had arranged for me to return to the Cold Storage Pad and Construction Camp 1.

My rationale was simple. I would not see Robert. I would be working seven twelve-hour shifts, and at the time, it paid thirteen hundred dollars a week. The three weeks I would work would take us through the summer until I could get a teaching job in the fall.

I had the most remarkable dream, or vision, really, that I went to Anchorage and spent time with someone like my good friend Freddie. When I was in the fourth grade, Freddie was my best friend in McCall, Idaho. It was a true egalitarian relationship and wonderful for both of us. Sometimes he was captain, and sometimes I played captain when we played "cavalry." We made every kind of fort we could think of as we chased around the vacant lot between our houses on Payette Lake. We were not Dylan Thomas's "king of the apple barns," but close. During my dream, my friend, like Freddie, and I stayed in a penthouse that looked out onto two skyscrapers.

I called Darrel, a good friend of David's and mine whom we knew from our days in Chugiak raising Siberian huskies. I was looking for a place for Robbie, Tim, and me to stay. Did he know of one?

Darrel had just returned to Alaska from Riverton, Wyoming, to work as a head of a private-sector correctional institution and had to leave his family behind until he was able to get a house for them in Alaska. The boys and I could stay with him until arrangements were made for the North Slope.

I sold my trusty Toyota truck and arranged for my stuff to be shipped as soon as I could pay for it. Darrel picked us up at the airport and took us to his penthouse that looked out onto two skyscrapers! He was very kind, and my relationship with him was much like the relationship I knew with Freddie in the fourth grade. I had actually seen the place we were going to in my vision—Darrell, the penthouse, the two skyscrapers. I was surprised, but I took it in stride.

Robert called and said he had made arrangements with the Teamsters Union. There were several things I needed to do. Since the Teamsters were limited to local hire, I had to buy a defunct car for the title and get some things to him like my old utility bills, to prove that I was an Alaska resident. He would take care of the rest.

I was questioning my sanity of going back to the North Slope, especially after Bruce's and Charlotte's reactions, so I went to the Anchorage Mental Health Center. I told them my story of the last eighteen months and asked them if there was a possibility that I was crazy. They conducted a series of tests, and an impressive series of psychiatrists and a psychologist reviewed everything, and their determination was that I was normal. I had an unusual experience, but I was still normal. I was relieved.

I called Bruce and Charlotte and told them what I had done and about the evaluation I had gone through. They thought it was funny that I went through all of that effort to prove that I was sane. They could have told me that. After seventeen years of being involved with the Cayce Foundation, Bruce said Edgar Cayce was normal. Why wouldn't I be? They could not, however, hide their concern about my pending employment.

Robert called and said that my five-week job on the North Slope was ready. Darrel found someone for Robbie and Tim to stay with. Darrel was, in a way, a spiritual teacher for a famous Alaskan artist, Jon. Jon had recently married his second wife, Charlotte, and they said they would love to take care of the boys to see if Jon would enjoy having children. It would just be for a short time, and they were good friends as well.

I was back on the North Slope, sick again after leaving Robbie. I went back to the Cold Storage Pad, worked my twelve-hour shift, ate in the cafeteria, went back to my dorm room, slept, and went back to work. I did the white light meditation and the automatic writing at night. Sometimes I would have very interesting guidance. When you have so many men and very few women, there is a lot of tension. The guidance said that I could use the light and surround the area with a sense of peace.

Being one of just fifteen women again with over four hundred men in Construction Camp 1, I couldn't hide. Men would come and sit near me and strike up conversations. I was polite but distant. It was not an easy time, but there was a kind man with whom I visited fairly frequently at dinner. He was in his fifties with a family in the San Francisco area and was one of the heads of the Bechtel Corporation on the North Slope. Bechtel was a major player in the construction of the Alaska Pipeline. Jim was his name, and he was not on the

slope on a permanent basis as many of the oil company executives were, so he was temporarily placed where the average
North Slope worker lived until an apartment opened up in
the management quarters.

I saw Robert periodically. He was distant, which was fine
with me, but he began behaving oddly, even more than usual.
I kept thinking about his talk of committing the perfect crime.
I wondered if he had not expected me to survive everything
over the last eighteen months. There was still a part of me that
hoped that he was not the man he was and that, magically, he
would become someone else.

The automatic writing continued to support whatever I
chose but began advocating my leaving the Slope. I returned to
Anchorage and my children, though I still did not have enough
money. I then made the mistake of my life and returned to the
North Slope for a final tour that was during Sea Lift.

The Sea Lift occurs during about two weeks in summer
when the frozen waterways of the Arctic Ocean thaw enough
so that the sea-going barges can bring their cargo to the large
community on the North Slope. Entire five-story-high buildings are loaded on barges in places like San Francisco, and they
make it to the docks at Deadhorse where they are offloaded.
Then those buildings, on giant tractor-like machines a quarter
of a block long, inch their way from the dock to their predes-
ignated position on specially made roads that can handle that
kind of tonnage.

Tim had flown back to stay with his dad for his summer
visit, and I arrived at Construction Camp 1 to begin my job
with the Sea Lift. Fortunately, even though everyone knew that
I was a "political appointee," the Teamsters Union members I
had worked with before had learned to trust me enough to give
me the job of driving pilot car. Leading those giant buildings

as they inched their way from the dock onto the roads and to their final destinations, sometimes in the fog, was fascinating but enormously stressful. The pilot car driver has to be sure that absolutely nothing is in the way of this entire process, as buildings, like the ones carried during Sea Lift, cannot be stopped.

Shortly after my arrival, I realized that Jim, my friend from Bechtel, was not there. Robert called me, and in the course of our conversation, he let me know that he knew Jim and I had become friends.

"Well, what happened to Jim? He's not here," I said.

"He's been fired," Robert replied.

"Fired? For what?"

"Nobody interferes with my property," Robert said matter-of-factly.

It gave me the chills.

"What? Who, pray tell, is your property?"

"I have to go now. Good-bye." Robert hung up the phone.

What? Did Robert have Jim fired because he was visiting with me? I had nothing to do with Jim but simple friendship, and how had Robert known we were visiting, anyway? I had never mentioned Jim to Robert once. Was this Robert's way of saying that I had better do whatever he wanted—that his power was unlimited and that he knew my every move?

That worried me. I had seen Robert some during my first visit to the Slope, but this time I just went to work and stayed away. I began thinking of leaving and just returning to my family. We had enough money to get by, and Sea Lift was almost over.

The automatic writing was encouraging me to leave as well. There was an ominous sense in the air. Robert was acting erratically, and I sensed that he was sneaking around and checking up on me, but I could not prove it. I was beginning to fear him.

I realized what a threat I was to him. Here I was, a woman who had just had his child. The company did not know about it. No one on the North Slope knew about it. I was acting as if nothing had happened, but that was nuts—just nuts, no matter what the Anchorage Mental Health Center had concluded about me. That was a rough crew in that cold, desolate place. What was I thinking? That everything was okay? If I were, I realized that I was just not thinking like Robert.

Then the final straw landed. One day, the writing looked eerily like Barbara McCormick's handwriting, and it was admonishing me to leave the Slope right then and said, "Do not wait. You could be in danger."

I plotted how to get off the Slope.

I made arrangements with personnel immediately and said that I had to leave for my family.

Leaving the North Slope

*You will see that the world is beginning to understand that
reality. It is beginning to move beyond fear, the pain, the
disasters, the theoretical earth changes, the tsunami, the
elements.... It is a shift in consciousness.*

−*The Immortal Now*

I am not a fearful person, but the fingers of fear were gripping me. I had no indicators, just a gut feeling like walking
through the woods and suddenly sensing something threaten-
ing before you round a curve and see an animal in the distance.
The feeling in the pit of my stomach told me that my beautiful
baby and I were in danger.

I left the North Slope, flew down from Deadhorse, and
went to pick up Robbie from his babysitter. I grabbed a cab,
knocked on the door of my kindly babysitter, and was led into
the room adjacent to where Robbie was playing. He was now
around a year old.

I stopped in the dining room and looked at Robbie in the
calico living room through the arch between the two rooms.
He was dressed in a light blue jumper suit with a yellow ducky
on the front. His beautiful blond hair was curly, outlining his
angelic, honest face with those twinkling brown eyes. He was
on his knees playing with a plastic red toy, absorbed in making
it work with his little Michelin tight arms. He looked at peace
but slightly frustrated by the toy.

He looked up and saw me and then looked at the toy I
had brought him. Both of our hearts leapt out of our throats.
I could feel it from his little baby body. He looked down at his

toy and then carefully looked back up at me to be sure that I was not an illusion.

"Hello, honey," I said. "It's Mommy."

He didn't respond. This time he stopped playing and just stared at the toy that had been absorbing his attention. It was obvious that he had felt great loss when I had left, and he was not sure that he wanted to trust me again. I just waited.

I knelt down on the floor at the entrance to the living room about three feet from him and just sat cross-legged waiting for him to see that I was still there. It was as though he said to himself, "Oh well!"

He stood up, looked at the toy in my hands, said, "Mommy!" and toddled over to me and into my arms. We both melted. I held all of that love close to me and breathed in his presence. I loved him more than my life or anything else at that point. I vowed that this was the last time that we would be separated in our lives together. My life was Robbie. He was my purpose, my sunshine, and separation from my son would now take an army.

A woman still on the North Slope subleased an Anchorage apartment to me. I paid the babysitter, and Robbie and I took a cab to our new, albeit temporary, home with Robbie clinging to my side like a baby monkey.

The apartment was part of a large, brown complex in the Muldoon area with its strip zoning and colorful signs. Ironically, it was about ten blocks from where I had met Robert three years before. It was close to large trees, and in order to enter, we had to go down a small tier of stairs. It had very little natural sunlight, but it was cheery and furnished with a floral couch and chair, the kind endemic to a second-hand store. There were rust-colored rugs in the living room covering a cement floor, a breakfast bar, a small kitchen, and one bedroom.

All that mattered to me was that I was with my baby. We played endlessly whatever he chose. I remember dancing to "Chariots of Fire" around the living room with Robbie. We played peek-a-boo and hide-and-seek but not as often as I would like because I sensed, when I would hide, that he was still worried about my leaving. Robbie had grown while I was gone, and we just had to catch up with each other.

About a week into our stay, I received a phone call from Robert. He said casually that he was just wondering where I had found a place to live. My heart stopped. How did he get this number? Did he find out from someone in the administration? Did the woman who subleased the apartment talk to him? What else did she tell him? Did she give him this address?

To my relief, he asked where I was living, so she had said nothing about the sublease. Or had she? I always had some sense of fear with him, but this time it was strong. His voice was too deliberately casual. He had no intention of seeing us. I made my excuses and hung up. I knew he had our number. The address would be next.

My body tensed. I would look around the apartment and at Robbie, and I couldn't see what was in front of my face. I was envisioning potential scenarios that could happen, and my fear blocked everything.

I sensed in my gut that he possessed the ability to have both of us killed without any remorse. I would not have thought that six months ago. I knew he was a compulsive liar, so I really didn't know what to believe. At one point, he had told me that he had been married to a woman in New Zealand, no details, and that he had killed her and had never been caught. Until now, I just blew that story off as a fabrication, but was it possible?

I was alone with my beautiful son and realized my family and friends didn't know where we were. If anything happened to us, only a few good friends and my teenage sons would know that Robert might have had anything to do with it. Robbie and I could suddenly just disappear, as was quite common in Alaska at that time. I knew by now that Robert was capable of anything, the more so with his position of power, his image as a family man and being an oil company executive. Who was I? And who was Robbie? How could I protect us?

All I could see before me was my worry and the images that they produced. I fed Robbie and put him to bed. I hardly slept that night. Adrenaline kept me going like a mother bear facing a rogue grizzly male in the darkness. I had been bold to go to the North Slope, and stupid, but now, either I was going to run, or I was going to face the situation head on.

In the book *Moby Dick*, one of my favorite chapters is entitled, "The Leeward Shore." In it, Melville states that in a storm the most dangerous place to be is what would otherwise be a safe harbor. The safest place was out at sea where the ship could not be plunged against its own moorings. So I fought all night to come up with a place that was "out at sea" for Robbie and me.

Filing EEOC Complaint

*You will see that you are not what you think. It will become
very clear in the near future. You are much, much more than
you can even try to imagine.*

—The Immortal Now

I finally decided that safety would be telling my story to someone in authority. I was long over being embarrassed by it.
Sharing what had happened to me on the North Slope and the
firing of a Bechtel executive and getting the entire story out
in some kind of public arena would ensure that Robbie and I
would survive. That was the point at which I decided to go to
the Equal Employment Opportunity Commission (EEOC) and
sue this major North Slope oil company for sexual harassment.

It was not easy. I looked up the EEOC and inquired about
where to go in a situation like this. When I called, the voice
of the employee at the other end of the phone said, "And how
may I help you?" I think she was expecting someone to ask for
directions to the office.

I timidly said, "I'm concerned about my life and the life of
my child. I need to report a sexual harassment situation on the
North Slope of Alaska."

There was a long silence at the end of the phone. Then she
said, "May I please put you on hold? I will need to make an
inquiry about this phone call."

"Thank you," I replied.

That week, after explaining my situation to several people,
I found myself with an appointment in person to discuss the
situation to an EEOC officer. I left Robbie at a friend's house,

dressed up, and summoned up all of my courage and determination to keep the appointment I had made with the lady on the phone.

I was shown into a large conference room and sat at the end of the table that had been designed for other things. A neatly dressed Filipina woman sat with a tape recorder in front of her. I remember feeling small and helpless. Some of our institutions are inadvertently intended to save lives. This one did.

"Now, all you have to do is tell all of your story from beginning to end into this recorder," the EEOC officer said. "If you need more tape, I have extra cassettes."

It took several hours while I struggled to find words for everything. Crying, I continued in spite of my impulse to run and thinking that it all just sounded like a soap opera—an oil-company-in-Alaska soap opera, a gut-wrenching, trying-to-find-God soap opera, a life-threatening soap opera. Everything that mattered was on that little black tape recorder with that frail hand pushing the buttons in an act of kindness and concern for another human being.

Finally, I had told the whole story, but something in me had changed. It reminded me of our session on the Source with Bruce. I had told a story that was at a level of consciousness that Bruce experienced when he did his taxes. What had happened in my life had come out of the decisions I made from the range of unlimited possibilities. It was as if I was in the middle of the play that was my life.

My decisions also put me in this room with this person at this time. It was I, but it wasn't. I was also at another level of consciousness where part of me was the love to the millionth power I experienced when I died, and I felt compassion for the people involved in the truthful story I had just told. Somehow, I knew that those words could, if I chose to use them, protect me and the child I loved so much. The aborigines of Australia have spoken of one's life being the dream and the story. This was mine on all levels.

The woman asked me if I wanted to file the complaint right away, and I said that I would think about it and get right back to her. In the meantime, could they get the complaint ready to file?

While all of the typing and creating of the complaint was going on, I was out looking for another apartment. I was concerned about Robert.

With little money, I found a place with a great landlady, Julie, who became a dear friend. I answered an ad for a one-bedroom apartment in downtown Anchorage. I dressed up in suit and heels, hoping to favorably impress the landlady. Julie rented it to Robbie and me right away. I think she loved Robbie most of all.

The place was so dirty that there was even a dried dog turd in the bedroom. I took it anyway. They did not need a deposit, and I am a compulsive cleaner, so immediately I cleaned the apartment, got my stuff out of storage, and went job hunting. I was so strapped for money after renting the apartment that I had to go straight with Robbie on my hip to the interviews.

I landed a job at Akeela House as a drug and alcohol counselor in a Synanon model of treatment. I was a little insecure about my suitability for the position. I would be running a confrontational group experience for fifty live-in, recovering alcoholics and addicts known as the "Synanon Game." Outside of a past stint working in a women's prison, I seemed unqualified, but with full immersion in the job and caring about the individuals I was dealing with, I could keep my head above water. I pulled it off. The problem was that I worked from 10:00 P.M.

until 2:00 A.M. Julie watched him in the evening when I was at work. I was exhausted in the morning when Robbie woke up.

Robert Finds Me

*The peace you seek is not in the mirror and
is outside of what you believe.*

–The Immortal Now

Out of the blue, Robert called again and said that he wanted to come see Robbie and me. In less than an hour, he knocked on the door of our new apartment. I tried to remain calm, debating with myself whether my fears were unfounded.

From the moment he walked into the room, he behaved oddly. He never smiled or really greeted me. He walked right past me and looked at the bedroom and at the bathroom. I expected him to say something. Robbie followed him around, and Robert paid no attention him. Then he turned to me, muttered something, and left as abruptly as he had arrived.

I felt as if he were casing my apartment and thought that if my fears were right, I was risking everything by staying quiet.

That was it! I called his wife in Idaho and told her that Robert had a son. She had no idea that Robbie existed. I had never wanted to hurt her in any way, but I was protecting my child—no more myths.

Then I called the EEOC.

"Yes, please file the complaint right away, if you would. Thank you for all of your help."

EEOC Complaint Hits the North Slope

When the world longs for peace, it truly longs for it within the individuals. It is a spiritual goal, not a group goal, so world peace is not possible. What is possible is individual peace, and the world reflects that individual peace.

−The Immortal Now

Word of the EEOC complaint on the North Slope spread like wildfire. Robert was not a loved figure there, particularly among the union members, though he was very popular with their leadership. There was hardly any difference between the Teamsters Union and oil company management at the top levels during that period of Alaskan history. Having spent a great deal of time with both, in Robert's presence, I observed that the union and corporate managements scratched each other's backs constantly. That was how I was able to work Sea Lift, a sought-after, well-paying tour.

I had also been privy to conversations among the oil company executives that they were interested in breaking the union. When are they not? A trucking company, K & W, had become competitive with the Teamsters and were simply more effective. I experienced this first-hand.

When I worked at the Cold Storage Pad for a short time after the Sea Lift, my fellow union members admonished me not to work so hard. I was a healthy, hard-working woman so when the time came to move the parts department for the heavy equipment they used in the oil fields, I did the work of two. Fellow union members told me that if I worked slower, the job could require two workers. I told them that if they did not put out their best efforts, Teamster Union jobs were someday going to disappear from the Slope. Old Teamsters, however, were so set in their ways that they could not hear. Not surprisingly, within six months, the Teamsters Union no longer had a presence with this oil company on the North Slope.

So with the union issues and the EEOC complaint afoot, Robert was not popular. His stock began to wane in the eyes of almost everyone. Graffiti appeared with expletives, taking his name in vain, according to some of my friends there.

The oil company did not let on that they were concerned about my EEOC complaint, but Robert was one of the vice-presidents of labor relations, no less, and appearance was key at the executive level. There were two vice-presidents in charge of labor relations. When one was on the Slope, the other was on R & R. Oil company management did not want to be crippled by a scandal with one of their top people and appeared to lend him support.

As the EEOC presented my story and negotiated with the oil company's attorneys, I believe I gained the distinction of becoming the first woman to sue a North Slope oil company for sexual harassment. Because of the previous relationship with Robert and our child, Robbie, the case was not classic in nature, and the harassment charges only concerned the second tour there.

What seemed like forever was, in fact, several weeks as we waited for the results of the EEOC investigation. My "out to sea" scheme from *Moby Dick* worked, or so I thought. Robert could not touch us, and danger was at bay for now.

Finally, the EEOC called and told me to come back to the same place that I had been interviewed. It was a gray, three-story building that looked like an IBM punch card.

"I'm sorry that we just don't have enough evidence to pursue this issue further," she said.

The words had an echo to them, and my heart stopped momentarily. I thought of all we had been through and watched with dry eyes the mouth of the small woman making this pronouncement.

If there is not enough evidence here, I thought, then when would they have enough evidence to pursue this issue?

"If you wish to pursue this further, you are going to have to get a private attorney and take it to a court of law."

I asked what turned out to be the most germane question. "And what attorney is going to take a case by a woman against this megalith oil company?"

The Search for an Attorney

*All life is moving beyond a death, generational, fear-based
paradigm. It is no longer within the head. It is within the
heart. It is difficult for you to imagine a world you know
now, free of fear. It is a challenge for you at this time.*

–*The Immortal Now*

Getting an attorney to sue a mega-corporation in Anchorage, Alaska, is, to say the least, an interesting challenge. However, the writing said that I would find an attorney.

I began by asking EEOC for potential lawyers. If you believe that the government is impartial in meeting out justice, you may not know enough about human nature. I truly believe that the EEOC meant well and had idealists on board with their organization, but this needs to be read in context.

Ronald Reagan had just been elected in 1981, regulatory enforcement was not priority one, and big oil companies were on a roll. In addition, there is every probability that this major oil company did not see the EEOC claim against one of their executives coming and was not prepared for the announcement that reached every worker on the North Slope. But that does not mean that they did not go right to work on skilled damage control.

Getting to the governmental leadership would have been one of their first tasks. I think it more than likely that the little Anchorage office of the EEOC did answer in some form or another to higher-up "contacts." It showed. So when I asked about lawyers, the EEOC backed off on making any kind of recommendation. I was on my own.

One of the first attorneys I went to was Robert's old partner, Paul, a flamboyant Anchorage attorney who, at one point, had been attorney general for the state of Alaska. When Robert graduated from law school in North Dakota, he went to work as an attorney in Anchorage under Paul. It was not long lived, however.

According to Robert, he was put on a criminal case, which was unusual for new lawyers. The trial was that of a massage parlor murder. In 1972, Wesley Ladd was accused of murdering a man named Ferris Rezk. Ladd was acquitted in spite of eyewitness testimony. Robert had bragged to me that he had the murder weapon in his safe during the trial and did not disclose it because "they didn't ask for it." Of course, they, the opposing attorneys, did not suspect that Robert had it since he would have been obligated to disclose that fact were he to follow any legal, ethical code. But Robert disclosed nothing and got Ladd off scot-free.

It was only when Robert's then ex-client committed another murder in 1973 that the Alaska judicial system found out about Robert keeping the murder weapon in his safe during the first trial. Ladd was found guilty of at least the second murder. Robert tried the first case without having passed the bar, so after the Alaska legal community realized what had happened, according to Robert, they approached him at the famous Petroleum Club, ironically, and told him that what he had done with the murder weapon was now common knowledge, and, "Oh, by the way, if you take the bar in Alaska, you will never pass." He never took the bar.

So Robert never practiced law in Alaska, but he did use his legal background in working for Alaska Constructors, which built the multi-million-dollar gathering stations on the North Slope during the feeding frenzy of the Alaska pipeline construction.

So here I was, headed to Robert's well-known ex-partner's office. I figured he should at least be informed of the situation Robert had created. Paul was a wonderful, heavy-set man, and I can still remember the smile on his face when I told him the story. He had questions about Robbie and was kind, but declined.

The next stop was a man in a mismatching polyester suit whose office was just off Ninth Avenue in downtown Anchorage. He was short and pudgy and stood before a lightly curtained window that looked out on the park. He was at least one of the more forthright attorneys I talked to. He simply said to me, smiling,

"Even though you might have a case, Patricia, I have chosen to practice law in Alaska, and were I to sue this oil company in any way, my law practice would be over."

He explained condescendingly, "It wasn't just the oil company that would frown on a lawsuit like this. Every company in the state that did business with it in any way, shape, or form at all—which according to my calculations, is just about every business in the forty-ninth state—would do so as well. Thank you very much for thinking of me, but no."

I asked for a referral, and I think in most cases, the attorneys referred me to their enemies.

I finally went through the phone book and let my intuition rest on an attorney who might take my case. I found one and learned to admire this remarkable man more than any attorney I have ever met. We started to make progress.

The Lawsuit

The fear of lack, the fear of pain, the fear of sadness, the fear of sin, the fear of sorrow, the fear of all of the elements of what is called the World of Fear are only like the mist in the garden, and when the fog lifts, the fog is gone.

-*The Immortal Now*

The last attorney I called said, "Come on over to my office and tell me about your case."

"Yes!" I made an appointment to meet him the next day.

To save time, I took a copy of the EEOC complaint with me. His office in downtown Anchorage was on the main floor of a house with a couple of bedrooms upstairs. It was painted a soft beige color with white trim, and his sign was in the small lawn facing the street. I walked in, holding Robbie on my hip.

He was nice looking and had a slightly disheveled dark suit on with a tie. There was no receptionist as there had been with the other attorneys I had interviewed. He had pictures of his family and wife in his office. I apologized about having Robbie with me but explained that it was hard to find sitters and that he was the ninth attorney I had talked to and I could not afford sitters for the initial interview.

He smiled and said that he understood. He was young, smart, idealistic, and was about finding out the truth—and he was kind. A breath of fresh air.

I offered the EEOC complaint, and he took it but said, "I would rather you tell me what happened in your own words." I had to keep it short since Robbie was busy. Michael said that it was smart that I brought my son along. It kept me to the point.

When the interview was done, he said that he would take the case on contingency. He felt it was an important case and could add to decisions made about oil companies in Alaska.

I only had a few blocks to walk to get to my small apartment, and I think I floated all of the way home.

The next several months were busy. I was working. Robbie was still a baby, and every spare moment I had was devoted to the case. My attorney had proceeded with discovery, and one day, he called me into his office to see evidence that had been gathered by the oil company attorneys.

"Patricia, you may be surprised and even offended by this."

"Try me, Michael."

"I'm not sure whose side the oil company is on. It looks as if they might be leaning towards you, actually."

"How?"

"Take a look."

He opened a folder that contained the testimony of five women. Michael told me to take the time now to read the document. It was their interviews. In all five cases, Robert had been stalking them.

One woman, who was described as tall, brunette, and "very attractive" said that Robert would show up at her room in Construction Camp 1 and surprise her. She said that she was frightened by his attention and asked him to stop seeing her, but he persisted. In every case, it was a single, attractive, young woman that Robert was seeking out. Part of me did not want to hear what other women were saying.

Michael said that he was not sure why they had mounted a case against their own employee, but maybe they were more sympathetic to what I went through than they were letting on.

"However," he said, "don't assume that this will translate into a settlement. They might just be setting up a situation where they could fire Robert and still get off without paying you."

Shortly thereafter, Michael said that the company attorneys had called and said just about that. They did not mention firing Robert, but wanted to settle the case out of court. They were willing to settle for twenty-five hundred dollars and no further lawsuits, and they would pay my attorney's fees.

The case had gone on for long enough to be a drag on my wonderful attorney, and I knew his practice was limited. If I settled, the oil company would not bear grudges against Michael, and he would be paid for his hours.

THE SETTLEMENT

*The world is an arena in which the forces, in effect, are forces
that clash sometimes because of the belief systems that have
evolved over, what you term, a long period of time, but
actually, they evolved within each individual
who subscribes to those belief systems.*

−*The Immortal Now*

Two oil company attorneys from the San Francisco offices
flew into Anchorage and met with me. They were matter-
of-fact and said that they would offer twenty-five-hundred dollars as a settlement and pay the attorney fees. That would be
the end of it. Both men wore basic corporate suits, had grey
hair, and were small in stature. They spoke as robots except
for a slight twinkle in the grey-blue eyes of the more slender of
them. They had made arrangements with my attorney ahead
of time so it was almost as though we all were going through
rehearsed motions. If I wanted to take the case further, I would
have had to come up with money I did not have, and it would
have been beating a dead horse.

My most important objective of protection for myself and
my son had been achieved, and in an odd way, at least a small
measure of justice had been served. The truth had been told,
and things were no longer secretive. It seemed subtle, but it
spoke volumes to the workers on the North Slope, particularly
the women. In a sense, it was the age-old desire to have the
world judge on the merits of the case, not because someone
was harming another by utilizing secrecy. I was at peace and

free at last of the fear that he would harm me. Robert's "perfect crime" had not worked out so well.

Looking back, the meditation and guidance I was given gave me the clarity and perspective to speak my truth, pursue this claim, and protect myself and my child. I never chose that meditation. I didn't go to India. I was given it, and it worked.

Shortly after the oil company settled with me, word came down from the North Slope. Robert had been fired. I was encouraged by a friend to file for child support through the Child Support Enforcement Agency. That's when I learned that Robert and his wife had divorced. Robbie ended up receiving the same amount of child support as his two half-sisters received from the divorce settlement.

SECTION THREE

LOVE TO THE MILLIONTH POWER

I Raise My Children

You will see that the way is becoming so very clear to those
who are understanding the nature of the present time, the
nature of the truth of being the nature of their power as
individuals. It is like looking into a beautiful well of water
and seeing all that exists reflected back into your own eyes,
which, in fact, reflect back into the water.

–The Immortal Now

Tim returned to Anchorage from visiting his dad. We moved to an apartment with a large living room, and Tim attended Bartlett High School, juggling Advanced Placement classes, varsity soccer, and competitive skiing.

Chris stayed with his dad to attend his private school. When Walter was transferred to London with CNN, Chris went with him and graduated from the American School there. His PSAT scores gained him a small National Merit scholarship, and Harvard accepted him.

Chris loved Harvard and would visit us in Anchorage as often as he could. Robbie discovered his other big brother and was always hugging him. It was increasingly difficult for Robbie to have either of his brothers leave. He would just cry.

Tim was back skiing with the Alyeska Ski Team, and they were happy to have him. That meant driving to the ski hill every weekend or car-pooling and providing for some equipment. Thankfully, Tim had become good enough to be sponsored for most of his ski gear. I was stretched about as far as I could go working full-time at Akeela House, raising Robbie, and struggling to keep our head above water financially.

The glitch was that Alaska was so far away from the Lower 48. Tim was competing at the national level and commuting between, say, Colorado and Anchorage, which was not compatible with his school schedule. Bartlett did not consider skiing to be an official sport, so they would not allow Tim to be out of school for more twenty days. That meant he would not be given credit for the classes he was taking.

Then I received a phone call from my sister, Gretchen. Her husband of twenty years had fallen in love with another woman and told her that he was going to keep both relationships going and would decide which woman he would stay with in June. Gretchen was inconsolable and would call and talk for three hours in the middle of the night. Sensing the seriousness of what she was going through, I made myself available for her whenever she would call.

On top of this, I was looking for a new job that would pay me more money. I received word that I was hired by the Alaska Council on the Prevention of Alcohol and Drug Abuse as a statewide teacher/trainer in the Here's Looking at You program. It was a considerable salary increase, and I took it. I quit my job and had about a month's break before starting my new one.

Meanwhile, I was mildly curious about what was going to happen with the last two books—what format they would take and what they would say. I knew the third book was to be on alternative realities and the fourth would be on love, salvation, and soul mates. But at the time, I had this debate going on with the Universe. I was not going to be out on the limb, financially, as I was with the first two books. And I knew I needed to do something about getting my first book, *Passage from Fear*, published. But I told the Universe that, for the well-being of my family, I just had to have something that was better grounded.

I FIND SISTER WORKS

You will see that the world is ready to understand the image
on the mirror and what is real. It is willing to begin to
explore the reality of the nature of the individual and begin
to cease turning its head from the exploration of love,
of the heart, of the power of love.

−*The Immortal Now*

While I was working for the Alaska Council, I began read-ing a book, *Transformers: The Therapists of the Future*. It was remarkable to me in that it followed the same train of thought as *Passage from Fear* and *Passage from Karma*. About the same time, its author, Jacquelyn Small, came to Anchor-age as the keynote speaker for the state drug/alcohol conven-tion. I was still doing automatic writing and asked for guidance regarding the speaker. The writing said to go to the convention and give her a copy of *Passage from Fear* and give her my phone number.

Her noon keynote address was gripping, and I waited patiently in line to do as I had been told. She was a beautiful, dark-haired, petite woman, and I was a little embarrassed to do as the writing dictated, but I had such faith in the work that I was obedient. When I told her that I had been instructed to give her a copy of *Passage from Fear* and my phone number, she smiled and thanked me.

About four o'clock that afternoon, I received a phone call from Jacquelyn saying that she would like to meet with me. I happily met her at the restaurant at the Sheraton where she had given her noon address.

With sparkling eyes, she said to me, "Patricia, we are channeling the same source! No one knows that my work is channeled—no one!"

She showed me a chart she had been given by her Source and began to explain why. The chart showed the chakras of the body. Jacquelyn pointed to the second one from the top labelled "Intellectual."

"My work is on the intellectual level," she said, "and is easily accepted by the intellectual community. I don't say anything about it being a channeled work, and the reader thinks it's like any other book."

She pointed to the Compassion chakra at the top of the chart.

"Your work, *Passage from Fear*, is on the compassion level of consciousness, so it comes through you and is written differently."

She went through each of the levels and showed me some of the limits of each one. The limit of the compassion level, she explained, was over-identification with the suffering of others.

"I have one other thing to tell you, Patricia. There is another sister work that you do not know about, and the thing that will knock you for a loop is that her work, *Agartha, A Journey to the Stars*, was begun on the SAME DAY as *Passage from Fear*! Patricia, the same day, January 16, 1981!"

She had brought down the *Agartha* book from her room and showed it to me. It was true! The author, Meredith Lady Young, had been very open about her work being channeled and had included a narrative of her own experiences in conjunction with the narration given by the Source.

Jacquelyn and I left each other reluctantly. I had to get back to Robbie since I had a babysitter, and Jacquelyn had to prepare for the next day. The writing had been correct again, this time two years later. It had predicted the four "sister works" at the beginning of the writing, and now the details were being filled in. I didn't know what the fourth sister work was, but the writing said that it was the only work that would come through a visible channel. The public could begin to see, then, that almost everything inspired, such as the arts, music, and spiritual insights, comes through this kind of process. And, it's been happening since the beginning of time.

FIRING AND IRONY

*The illusion that exists that there is anything except the
present time, except the nature of the individual, except the
multiplicity of levels of understanding, except the beauty
within, is the illusion that is leaving your experience.*

–*The Immortal Now*

I had a poetry professor at the University of Washington
who used to encourage the use of irony in writing. I would
strongly discourage the use of irony in actual life, however; it is
too painful. I used to say that I didn't want anything ironic in
my life that wasn't funny. I was trying to hedge my bets against
reality, and it did not work. Somehow, serious irony may be
part of the fabric of life itself so, in order to change that, one
could no longer weave life's fabric at all.

With my increased income from my new job, it was time to
look for a house. I had been eyeing a small townhouse with a
lease/purchase agreement. I took it, and we moved in. It had the
smallest living room you have ever seen with an even smaller
fireplace. The kitchen, dining room, and bathroom were also
on the first floor. The upstairs had three sizable bedrooms,
which became our favorite place to land. We had a home of
our own.

Then I received a call from Gretchen—the same Gretchen
who had protected me from taking my own life with her ardent
prayers.

"Patty, are you sitting down?"

"Yes, as a matter of fact," I replied.

"Good."

"So, what is it Gretchen?"

Her voice became inordinately quiet.

"Patty, I am in a mental institution. They have brought me here for observation. Patty, I tried to take my life."

"What!"

"Kip finally told me that he decided to stay with Kathy and said he was getting a divorce. I just couldn't keep things going, so I took two hundred aspirin and jogged to get it going and headed to the woods to die. Someone saw me and stopped and began talking to me. He realized that everything was not quite right. He got me to help, and here I am in one of those nighties in some kind of ward."

"Gretchen!"

"Patty, it was just too much. It was just too much."

"Gretchen, I will find a way to get down there. We are going to do this together. You are going to be okay."

I got her number, hung up the phone, and spoke with my mother about Gretchen and asked to borrow some money.

"Why did she do a dumb thing like that?"

My mother's response shocked me. Did she not register what had just happened to her daughter? Gretchen had almost died, and were it not for a caring stranger, she would have. Well, no time to worry about that. I made arrangements for my family and then to go to Moscow, Idaho. I needed to do whatever I could to help my sister.

The Alaska Council had just gotten a large grant on suicide prevention since Alaska had one of the highest suicide rates in the United States. Irony upon irony, the director receiving this grant now firmly planted her feet staunchly and opposed my preventive act to go down and retrieve my sister. In her mind, prevention would be "enabling." I was dumbfounded. Enabling what—her life?

I had leave-time coming, so I took off and decided to bring my sister back to Alaska. I helped Gretchen pack up her stuff at Washington State University, which is near Moscow, Idaho. She wanted to be closer to Kip in an attempt to save their marriage. I met with Kip, who would not look me in the eye. Gretchen was not always that easy to live with, but she was loyal to a fault. They had loved each other since they had been fourteen years old.

Gretchen and I drove to Seattle. When we arrived at the Seattle airport, where we were going to leave her car with our cousin, Gretchen tried to give her favorite painting to me, which I refused. Then, she insisted on driving the almost twenty-four-hundred-mile Alaska Highway alone, instead of flying.

I panicked, but there was no dissuading her. I was as frightened for her as she had been for me just a few years earlier after the accident in London. I prayed constantly for the four days it took her to drive the Alaska Highway. Maybe Bruce McArthur was right in being puzzled about my coming back to Alaska. If I had stayed in the Lower 48, then I might have been closer to Gretchen through her whole ordeal and this would not have happened. The what ifs are always many.

The upshot was that Gretchen received professional help. For taking leave to help her, I was fired from my job the exact day—almost to the minute—one year after Robert was fired from his job on the North Slope. On top of that, the cause of her suicide attempt was that her husband had met someone else and decided to leave Gretchen and marry the other person. Brutal irony without an ounce of humor.

Bruce McArthur had published his book, *Your Life: Why It Is the Way It Is and What You Can Do About It*. Much of what Bruce had discovered in his years with the Edgar Cayce works was about Universal Laws of Cause and Effect: what is put out there is what comes back—the traditional sense of karma. Had getting Robert fired from his job come back to me by being fired from my job one year later?

But my near-death experience and the guidance in *Passage from Karma: A Coming Release from Sin and Repentance* taught me that there is only life, love, and unlimited possibilities in the present moment. You are released from karma. *Passage from Karma* said,

> *You will be free of your beliefs about karmic debt when you leave the World of Fear, my children, and will never return to them. For just as you learned to add and then went on to more involved concepts so it will be as you have mastered the base from which you are working.*

> *You are now ready to go into more advanced concepts about the nature of spiritual reality and will not need to master 2+2=4 again and will be ready for a spiritual calculus of being. You will retain the basic mathematics but will not dwell on it but rather dwell on the calculus with which you are working now.*

By using the meditation and asking for guidance, I learned that you can walk into healing situations, much as I had. It gave me a sense of hope that this would be possible for Gretchen, Kip, and even Robert.

Publication of the First Book: *Passage from Fear*

You will see that the way will become easier for all life.
It is like sliding down a beautiful stream in the sunlight.
It becomes easier as you go.
You simply become more lost in the present.

–The Immortal Now

After getting fired, I went to Bethel at the invitation of my loved chosen sister, Rosie. Robbie and I stayed in a temporary rental of Rosie's and wrote seventeen query letters to potential publishers about the first book. Two publishers responded and both would require money to publish it.

Philosophical Library had published Albert Schweitzer's books and had a long tradition of supporting cutting-edge philosophical works. They loved the book. The other respondent was Coleman Publishing in Long Island, a young company that had published *A Course in Miracles* and the works of a new author, Louise Hay.

Interesting. Our session on the Source about two years earlier had talked about *A Course in Miracles*. Nothing happens by chance.

Coleman Publishing was started by Saul Steinberg, a short, chunky, dark-haired businessman who was tighter than a tick with money. One time, Saul told me the funny story of how his publishing company began. He had a small printing business at the time. Someone came to him and said that he had been guided to tell him that he would be printing a book that which was a channeled work.

"I will?" Saul replied.

According to Saul, the person said that he would make a sizable profit with the book, to which he smiled and replied in his businessman's tone, "Yes, I will."

That was a happy day for him, he told me. With the publication of *A Course in Miracles*, Coleman Publishing was born.

I had stayed in frequent communication with Bruce and Charlotte McArthur. They decided to invest in publishing the first book through Saul Steinberg and Coleman Publishing and had settled on the title: *The Renaissance: From the World of Fear to the World of Love.*

After the book was published, Saul wanted me to come to San Francisco for the American Booksellers Convention at the Moscone Center and give out two hundred copies. First, though, Saul wanted me to spend three days with him at a workshop conducted by Louise Hay in Los Angeles.

My Uncle Ed had passed away and left me a small inheritance. I used it to buy a Volkswagen camper that Robbie and I could drive down to Los Angeles, then up to San Francisco, and on to Wenatchee for Tim's high school graduation.

I met Louise Hay and Saul for the first time at a Los Angeles hotel for the workshop. Saul was funny and, as he called himself, "a frumpy Jewish man," in contrast to the tall, slender, eclectic and well-dressed Louise Hay. Halfway through the workshop, Louise announced that five of the approximately twenty attendees had HIV/AIDS and that if any of us were queasy about it, we could consider leaving. Of course, no one left, but my heart went out to the struggle the individuals there were facing. We spent enough time together to care what happened to them and for me to be able see them always in my mind's eye. There was little hope for those with AIDS at that time.

After the workshop was over, Robbie and I went to Disneyland. Robbie was fiercely independent from birth—and funny! I had innocently taken Robbie to the movie *Pinocchio* just before we left for California thinking that it was a child's movie. So when we arrived in Disneyland, we started on the Pinocchio ride. I had not realized that Stromboli had scared Robbie during the movie. When we turned the corner on the boat and Stromboli jumped out, Robbie screamed as though he had just been attacked by a lion. I held him and calmed him down, but he was just mad—and he was mad at me for taking him on the ride and let his feelings be known.

We walked past Donald Duck, and Robbie toddled over to him, pulled on his tail feathers until he had Donald's attention, and said, "Do you know what my mommy did? She took me on the Stromboli ride and scared me!"

Then Robbie walked further down the sidewalk until he found Goofy and went right up to him and adamantly complained, "Do you know what my mommy did? She took me on the Stromboli ride and scared me."

How embarrassing!

Even on the train around Disneyland, he went up and down the aisles telling the other passengers about his mother's screw up.

On the way back to San Francisco, Robbie and I traveled up the Pacific Coast Highway. He discovered the ocean. He just could not leave the beach. He would cry and kick when I'd pick him up to leave, and he would tell me to go back.

"But, honey, Mommy has to go on to her meeting in San Francisco, and you can see Uncle Todd."

Robbie loved talking with my brother on the phone and giggled most of the time because Todd told silly, little kid jokes. Robbie turned my forty-something-year-old brother into a three-year-old.

Somehow, with more fun than you can imagine, Robbie and I made it up the glorious California coastline with this fresh new life taking in every starfish, piece of seaweed, light of sunset, and detailed gift of God.

We arrived in San Francisco, and Robbie and I stayed with Todd at his apartment in Pacific Heights. Todd would sit on the bed next to Robbie while the happy child watched the cartoon, "He-Man." Then they played together in the sandbox at the park across the street. My brother, who lived in one of the most impeccable high-rent apartments available and who had a debonair manner of dressing, came back to his apartment after frolicking with Robbie in sand-covered Calvin Klein's, which threw sand everywhere on expensive Oriental rugs.

"Man, what a great sandbox fight that was! Three-year-olds are what I want to be when I grow up!" he said with a big smile.

Passage from Fear, the print version now called, *The Renaissance,* said that the environment is within, and it could not have been seen more clearly than in the open eyes of Robbie. He was seeing thousands of things I had forgotten. His sensitivity to truly see so much was coming from within himself. He loved everything around him to the point that he did not want to leave it. *Passage from Fear* said that children are our teachers. I was Robbie's student. I was learning his enthusiasm, his love, his joy, and his presence in the Presence—laughing, running, playing, and taking it all in.

I could see the World of Love the books talked about in Robbie. Through him, I felt the love to the millionth power, which I had experienced when I had died, taking me out of the World of Fear.

The books said that children were "only a window through which you can look at your own massive, spiritual identity." The books were right. Their messages could not be contained within their covers. Rather, they were bursting out from the writing now in every minute of my experience. They were like sunlight out of the clouds, and my life was turning into a sunburst.

The fourth book on love, salvation, and soul mates—the one you are reading now—was being written, but I was unaware of it at the time. I could feel that light, that love, and that peace better, only it was occurring within me. It really was not in a book I had read before, or in an organization, or a religious tradition—or with a man. The heart felt like home, and it was disclosing itself in its own way, writing its story in the love of everyone I loved with all of my heart. *Passage from Fear* said,

> *As your thought expands, you will pull out of a dream state that you have been in for many thousands of years…. . You will find that when you cross that chasm out of the world of fear, you will walk like a glowing man into blinding light and will love that light and find that that light permeates everything and, in fact, always has, so that the things—tangible objects that you have assumed were tables or chairs or houses or whatever—were ultimately comprised of light itself.*

I met Saul Steinberg and Louise Hay at the Moscone Center. If you have never been to the American Booksellers Convention, the most apt description you can give it is that the circus has come to town! There were hundreds of booths by publishers trying to sell their books, each trying to outdo the other.

As you passed the romantic book section, handsome men in dashing costumes and beautiful women seduced bookstore owners into fake palace-like displays to open the world of fantasy to potential customers. There was color, dancing, almost carnival-barker selling of the latest novel. It was just fun, and the person who loved it most was Robbie. He was smitten with everything going on around him and kept toddling off to see something or find another bear or book or child somewhere. Bookseller conventions are mostly made for the child in us all.

Louise Hay and I watched the Coleman Publishing booth where she expressed concern about the snail's pace at which her books were coming out and said that she was thinking of starting her own publishing company. I remember thinking what a good idea that was and wished I could do that as well, but then there was Robbie. Most of my time was spent trying to catch my three-year-old.

I did a book signing on the other side of the center across from Geraldine Ferraro, our first female vice-presidential candidate. I realized that as much as I wanted to devote all of my time to getting out the two remarkable books that had been created, *Passage from Fear* and *Passage from Karma*, I could not. Life itself was calling me in Robbie, along with everything else that was pressing. It took every ounce of energy I had available just to participate in that World of Love that was opening up for me.

Robbie and I said our good-byes to my new brethren, Saul and Louise, and to San Francisco. We made it to Wenatchee and Mission Ridge Ski Academy the day before Tim's graduation and stayed with Tim's host family.

Tim hardly had any time for us. His life had become the Mission Ridge Ski Academy world, and both Robbie and I were disappointed in not seeing him more. But, what did we expect?

Tim was in the middle of a dilemma, to which I was not privy. Should he take a year off to focus his entire energy on making the U.S. Ski Team, or should he go ski for the University of Colorado? He had just beaten several Olympians and was on a roll. If he was going to take a ski year, it was going to be up to his dad to pay for some of it. Walter wanted Tim to go to college and was afraid that if Tim took a year off he might not finish his education. The decision was made for him to go to college.

Unaware of Tim's dilemma and the decisions being made between him and his father, Robbie and I headed back to Alaska. If I had known, I would have stayed and fought for Tim to have that opportunity. Unfortunately, opportunities like the U.S. Ski Team rarely come along twice.

Robbie and I managed to find every water slide we could in southern British Columbia on the way. Seven hundred miles out of Whitehorse, our camper broke down. A wonderful couple ended up towing it behind their truck with a cab-over camper. It ended up carrying three adults, Robbie, their three children, and four dogs. We made it, had the camper fixed in Fairbanks, and took off for our townhouse in Anchorage.

Tim came back to Alaska to pack for college, and Robbie and I took him to the airport to go to Colorado. Then the trauma of Robbie's young three-and-a-half-year-old life occurred. Tim flew off in what Robbie disdainfully called the "big airplane." We hadn't anticipated the effect on Robbie's young heart. It was broken. He couldn't sleep. He was up at four in the morning and would toddle into Tim's room to see if he was there. No Tim. Then he would come back to me, palpably angry, and say, "Why did that big airplane take my Mimmy? I did not want it to take him. Mommy, bring Mimmy back!"

Robbie was not kidding! He meant for me to take care of this untenable situation. Period! We thought it would subside in time, and eventually it did, but the early morning routine continued for almost a month. Robbie was inconsolable. Tim was simply too important in his life.

ON TO FAIRBANKS

You will see that the heart is not only the center of the individual; it is also a window to the universe. It is difficult for you to understand at this point that when one talks of space travel or other ideas that they simply do not originate in the intellect.

—The Immortal Now

I received a call from a good friend, Isabella Tweedy. It is interesting where you meet soul mates. Before David entered graduate school in seabird studies at the University of Washington, I worked as a counselor in the drug/alcohol section of a minimum-security prison in Purdy, Washington. There, I met Isabella Tweedy, half of what she called the notorious "Tweedy Gang."

Isabella, at fifty-six, had been dying of chronic-stage incurable alcoholism. She and her sixth husband, Emmett, had used toy guns to hold up a place outside of Spokane. They made it about four hundred feet before they were arrested, and both received five-year sentences.

Isabella had been a prodigy as a child, reading Chaucer at eight years old. She had written poetry all of her life and had boxes of her most treasured possession, her poetry, in her prison room. We became fast friends, and after some encouragement, she decided to get her GED, and then took the CLEP test, which is a college equivalency exam. Isabella blew the lid off the test.

I wanted to show Isabella's poetry to my favorite professor at the University of Washington, Nelson Bentley, a peer of

Theodore Roethke. Isabella was terrified the day I picked up her boxes.

"Isabella," I said, "they are only words."

"It would be easier were you to take one of my arms or my legs," she replied in disbelief.

The result was that Isabella was accepted into the Resident Release program as an undergraduate at the university, with Nelson Bentley's help. She taught mysticism in the philosophy department and finished her bachelor's degree with a 4.0, of course. Isabella followed it with a master's degree and her Ph.D. I always said that knowing Isabella was like being friends with Gertrude Stein.

When Isabella learned that I had lost my job, she called and wanted me to move to Fairbanks. There was a job at the Fairbanks Correctional Center as a drug/alcohol counselor, and she thought I might be able to help her start a private drug/alcohol treatment center. It all worked out as she had hoped. We started the Milam Recovery Center and then the Horizon Recovery Center after I worked at the jail.

Then I had another premonition. My mother had been living at a retirement home and was moved to a nursing home in Billings, Montana. Mom was carefully cared for by my sister, Bonny, who truly was her best friend. Bonny called me to say that Mom was not doing well. It hit me, as it always did, and I realized that my mother would pass on within a month. I was tired of knowing these things were going to happen and not acting on that information. I called everyone who loved her and said to go see her now.

I flew down with Robbie, and he had a chance to meet his grandmother for the first time. She was not communicating, but when I walked in the room and announced that Robbie was there, she smiled. The writing may have been right that my mother had killed me in another life. It does not matter. I do know when the light of love enters a room, the darkness—wherever it might have come from—goes away, and one does not even worry where the darkness went. I had loved my mother unconditionally with all of my heart, all of my life.

Master's Degree

*That is the nature of present time because there is no time
anywhere, at all, under any circumstance.
Time is a fabrication. It is a deception.*

−*The Immortal Now*

I decided to get my master's degree in educational administration and entered graduate school at the University of Alaska.
I had not worked in teaching, my chosen profession, since
Robert had entered my life. To provide better for my family, I
knew I needed the graduate degree to be a principal/teacher, a
position common in rural Alaska. Besides, I loved it!

I was continuing to use the white light meditation daily, as
the writing had encouraged me, and had come to terms with
the fact that my path was not going to be like that of Louise
Hay and others. Their books were becoming part of main-
stream America. The writing had told me that I was destined
to write four books and that they were to come out thirty years
after the first one began—January 16, 1981.

My path was to use the white light meditation, knowing intuitively that my job was to raise the children I adored.
Whatever the Universe had in store was okay with me. It would
work out in its time. I was beginning to understand that our
lives are perfect and to trust the wisdom and intelligence that
was coming from the love within my heart. The love to the millionth power was showing up everywhere, and I was following
it like a plant following sunlight. I could catch that love in only
a glimpse at a time, but each as intense in milliseconds as it had
been when I had died.

With Robbie in kindergarten, I went back to school full-time. Chris was going full swing at Harvard and came out for Christmas to enjoy the northern lights and the science being gathered about them by the Poker Flats Research Station. Tim was skiing at the University of Colorado. I was still working part-time with Isabella.

Off to Holy Cross and the Alaskan Bush

*You will see the connectivity of all life more and more
clearly. You will begin to see the ebb and the flow of the
consciousness of each individual connecting with each other
individual so that as the individuals create the flower or
begin to create, together, the ascension, the relationship
becomes more and more connected.*

−*The Immortal Now*

About two-thirds of the way through my master's program, an opportunity showed up to work again in the bush. Salaries were good, and it was easier to get back into a teaching position there. I interviewed for an "everything" job in the village of Holy Cross on the Yukon River. Little did I know that teaching in this small remote Native village would expand my spiritual teachings into other cultures. I was going to be working with Martha, a woman I came to know as a soul mate when I was doing research for the Alaska Council on the Natural Helpers program in rural Alaska.

I had learned to love the Yup'ik Eskimo language from my Foxfire project days in Bethel. Now I would learn Deg'hitan Athabascan Indian as well. Holy Cross was a juncture of both distinct cultures.

During that project, I had flown all over interior Alaska, from the village of Red Devil on the mighty Kuskokwim to Kwethluk, and interviewed Native elders on traditional ways of helping. I also went to a conference at the University of Alaska for the gathering of traditional Native healers from around the planet.

Passage from Fear had frequently talked about healing, and when I attended the conference, its messages seemed so close to what those healers believed. Of special interest was a Lakota healer from a reservation in South Dakota, Joseph Eagle Elk, and his sidekick (which healers often have), Stanley Red Bird. Jerry Mohatt, who put the conference together, had spent nine years with Joe Eagle Elk and wrote a wonderful book on Joe's experience of becoming a medicine man, *The Price of a Gift*.

A traditional Lakota healing ceremony was going to be at Jerry Mohatt's house. I wanted to go, but I had my child. I went to Jerry's house to make my apologies.

"I'm sorry, Jerry, but you do not want an active child in your important ceremony."

"Yes, we do, Pat. Children always come, and you will see that he will do great. Please bring him."

Later I learned that they were doing the ceremony for Martha, from Holy Cross, who had terrible rheumatoid arthritis.

"Okay, Jerry. I will be bringing my sister as well." Gretchen was visiting me in Fairbanks.

We arrived at the ceremony and were sitting on the floor of Jerry's basement. The windows were darkened with aluminum foil and Robbie was in my arms, and we were two persons away from Martha.

Robbie looked at me and said, "Mommy, I tho scared. I tho scared."

I was beginning to think that my worst fears were right. This was no place for a child. But when Joe came in and started the ceremony, Robbie relaxed in my arms and remained so for an astonishing two hours. It was a miracle!

I met Martha, and like true soul mates, we loved each other from the start. She was from the Aleutian Islands and was around five feet two inches tall with the beautiful body and rich, dark skin of the Aleut people. Martha was a master of translation from one culture to the next. At the age of forty-seven, she had gone back to school to become a teacher for her village.

Right after I got the job to teach in the elementary and high schools, Robbie and I flew to Holy Cross and moved into the tiniest apartment I had ever lived in.

Holy Cross is a small village of around two hundred Yup'ik and Deg'hitan Athabascans, which was originally huddled along the Yukon River before it wandered several miles away like an errant child. The land around the village is largely tundra, but the area around Holy Cross has evergreens and some deciduous trees.

Catholic missionaries first went there to establish an orphanage to house the hundreds of Native children whose parents had been killed by the flu epidemic of 1918 and the diseases brought along the Iditarod trail. The village of Holy Cross had been "selected" by the Catholics. The Catholic, Moravian, Quaker, and Russian Orthodox Catholic missionaries all sat down together and decided which village would be converted to which religion, and they agreed not to infringe on each other's territories.

The missionaries were puzzled why the Holy Cross Natives had placed their village on the other side of the river and not where the missionaries eventually built their church, in the nice flat space with a small mountain near it. Later, they found that they had placed the Catholic Church over ancient burial grounds, which is why it was flat!

Shortly before coming to Holy Cross for my job, Alaska had just settled what is known as the Molly Hootch case, which enabled all of the small villages in rural Alaska to build their own new schools. Prior to the case, bush Alaskan kids had to leave their homes and go to regional high schools. Because they were not parented during their teen years, we were facing a generation who did not really know how to parent teens. The elders of the village and the whole community stepped in to make education effective. Robbie went to first grade there, and I taught some sixth-grade classes and, with Martha, high school English, along with economics, art, and whatever else was needed.

We Almost Lose Robbie

It is critical for you to understand that the mirror is not all there now because the mirror is losing its charm for you and your need is to return more and more to your home, to your consciousness, to your being, to your soul, to yourself, and to the love that binds you with all life.

—The Immortal Now

I loved teaching in bush Alaska, but mid-year, Robbie broke his femur in a sledding accident. Were it not for the quick thinking and protectiveness of the village health aide, Frieda, I might have lost my wonderful son. The men of the village wanted to pick up Robbie and load him onto a sled. Frieda ran between Robbie and the men and stopped them. She then facilitated the process of correctly loading him into a sturdy basket where the leg would not move as his jagged bones could have severed the femoral artery. We nearly lost him.

It was night when we loaded Robbie and me on a small plane to Bethel where he was transported by ambulance and placed into a freight box. Robbie was raised by a forklift onto the jet for Anchorage while I watched from the ground before climbing the steps to get into the plane. Six seats had been put down to handle the basket in which he had been placed. Sixteen hours from the accident, we arrived at the hospital in Anchorage and had the leg set and casted.

Outside of the London accident, it was the greatest night of terror that I had experienced. Then the Iditarod School District told me I had to go back to the village for three days in order to keep my job and health insurance. This meant that

I had to leave my baby boy behind. Robbie was terrified the whole time, in traction, with muscle spasms, and wondering where his mommy went.

When Robbie's leg was finally put into a cast, he and I flew back to the village in a ten-seater airplane. For Native people, flying like a tiny mosquito being batted about by the wind was a matter of course. With no roads to speak of in rural Alaska, small airplanes were the basic mode of transportation, even to adjacent villages. For other passengers on that plane ride back from Anchorage, it was a chance for a nap. For Robbie and me, it was a chance to lose our lunch almost the entire way.

Martha met us at the airport and took us to our little red house on the hill we had moved into after our tiny apartment became too small. The other reason we moved out of our apartment was that it was not soundproofed, and Rob's first grade teacher had just gotten married, and we could hear everything their late evening activities could produce. First grade was too early for sex education. Time to move.

Our new "Molly Hooch" school had opened. It was a large and contemporary building, holding grades pre-school through twelve. With an open center in Arctic blue and mauve overtone, it was ADA compliant, but meant for adults. The Principal/Teacher of the school, Steve, was a blond, harsh man, about six feet tall. He acted as if he liked the kids, but they knew better.

Frustrated, Robbie was learning to manage a wheelchair, also not meant for children, with his cast out in front of him like a knight's lance. He did the best he could, but it was not easy. At one point, Robbie was trying to maneuver his nemesis-chair around a short turn after just ascending a too-steep handicapped ramp. He accidentally ran into the wall on the outside of the Principal/Teacher's office and left a one-inch mark where the metal of the wheel leg brace dug into sheet rock. Steve emerged from his cave, livid, and yelled at Robbie. Robbie's face was white, and he was trying not to cry.

Emerge champion Martha onto the scene. Martha, with her soft, melodic Native accent, which can only be described as a thoughtful cadence, took on the role of guardian angel and spokesperson for Robbie. Shocked at Steve, she took her five-foot-two-inch frame, almost tiptoed to make herself larger, and placed herself between Robbie and Steve.

She looked at him with dark eyes sparkling with restrained outrage. "Ooooh. Steve. Shame on youuuu, Steve! He is a child, and he is trying his best to manage an impossible situation."

Robbie relaxed.

Then she turned to Robbie and said, softly, with all of the love she felt for him, "Robbie, did you make that hole in the wall? What a wonderful hole, Robbie! It shows just how courageous you are to try to make that turn."

Some of the students had gathered around shyly. She turned to them and said, "You need to know that I will always honor that hole. I don't want it fixed. It shows just how difficult it has been for our little friend and how hard he's tried to deal with what he has been through."

Steve disappeared back into his office.

Then she turned to Robbie and said, "Come on, Robbie. I'll push you to class this time." Robbie always loved Martha.

Spring arrived, and Chris was graduating from Harvard, but I could not attend because of my job. Martha decided to go to Harvard in the fall to earn a Master's Degree in Cross Cultural Education. She later became an international spokesperson for Native Americans across the United States and Canada. After nearly losing Robbie, I vowed, right then, that I would get a job in town.

Interestingly, it was during my time in Holy Cross when I discovered the fourth sister work, *A State of Mind: My Story/ Ramtha: The Adventure Begins,* the one that the writing said was to be by a visible channel, JZ Knight.

I taught one more year in rural Alaska and was transferred to the village of Takotna, population forty-seven, including the children. Takotna is 150 miles north of Denali, and the Iditarod runs through town. I taught preschool through twelfth grade and was the principal for this $1.5 million school for sixteen kids.

The educational experience was everything I had ever dreamed of, if a little cold. It was unofficially recorded to minus 87 degrees, the coldest temperature recorded in the North American continent, and it never warmed up any more than minus 70 for three weeks. Everything in the village froze up except the school, and I kept school going.

Most of the children lived near the school except for one family with four children. Getting their books to them was a challenge. Vehicles cannot be driven at that temperature because some metal can become brittle and fracture, and dogs cannot be run, or their lungs will freeze. A local musher walked his dog team and carried the books to their house four miles from town. I would call on a CB radio and discuss the lessons for the day. The children were home-schooled through the cold spell and checked in with me by CB periodically for help.

The following summer, Robbie and I moved back to Fairbanks where I finished my master's work through the University of Alaska.

Town Looks Great

It is like a renaissance. It is like a breakthrough. It is the moment at which the chicken emerges from the egg and discovers the world beyond the egg. That is what is happening within consciousness at this point.

—The Immortal Now

I had saved my money, made sure my credit was improved, and at last found a teaching job in Fairbanks. Early in my master's program, I had done my principal's internship in Fairbanks for a wonderful man who ended up hiring me for a position at North Pole Middle School. I bought a beautiful twenty-seven-hundred-square-foot house on the Chena Slough in North Pole, a moose habitat, and moved in on Christmas Eve with Robbie, the visiting Chris, and a good friend, Patricia.

The next eight years were spent raising Robbie, seeing Chris and Tim whenever I could, and hosting four exchange students: Ernesto from Monterray, Mexico, Soren from Odense, Denmark, Edi from Finland, and Yvgeney from Yakutsk, Siberia. I had settled in my beautiful home but often wondered about the writing's statement that I would do two more books: alternative realities and love, salvation, and soul mates. It also said that the world needed them and they were to help prepare for 2012 and the next hundred years.

I continued to use the white light meditation, and in the back of my mind, I was having conversations with myself and reminding the Universe that I would continue the work if I had a stable home, income for my family, and safety for my sons. I liked the warm home with the predictability and reasonableness of my life, and my children were flourishing. That was the deal with the Universe—possibly negotiable, but a wish list if it wouldn't mind too much, please, please.

THE LOWER 48

*What you see and what you experience as an image is what
has occurred because, to truly be in the present time,
you do not exist within the image.*

—*The Immortal Now*

In 1996, I learned that I had endometrial cancer, and within a
week, I flew to Seattle with Rob and was gutted and neutered
in one fell swoop. The hysterectomy took everything remotely
female, and I was safe. I realized that I did not want to go back
to Alaska with my son as it was too far away from extended
family, especially Tim, who was living in Seattle.

When Alaska offered an early teacher's retirement, I
jumped at it and decided to move to Port Angeles, Washington. It's a community I had loved since teaching on the Makah
Indian Reservation in Neah Bay twenty-four years earlier. It all
made sense—logically.

Port Angeles is ninety miles west of Seattle on the lush
Olympic Peninsula. It is a jewel on the Straits of Juan de Fuca,
for it is near the rain forest but in the rain shadow, created by
the Olympic Mountains. Crescent Lake, with its turquoise
water mirror reflecting giant cedar trees, is to the west.

I rented a beautiful four-bedroom home near Port Angeles High School. Rob played basketball and then decided to
become a Rotary Exchange Student to Germany the next year.
Before we moved to Port Angeles, he and I had looked at one of
my favorite homes on the main street coming from the Victo-
ria Ferry. We thought about making it into a bed and breakfast
and thought that with its income combined with my limited

retirement income, I would do well. It did not work out. I needed a teaching job to make ends meet, and there were none to be had. I was substitute teaching, and it was not enough to get by on financially.

Enter my chosen sister, Rosie, who had sold her newspaper and everything she owned in Alaska and had been living in an RV for eight years. She was headed for Palm Springs, California. Chris and Tim were grown, and Rob was off in Germany. Hallelujah, I was a bum!

Rosie helped me decide to get my own RV and follow her to Palm Springs. I sold my house in North Pole that I had been renting, bought my RV, and put my belongings in storage. The writing said that there would be two more books. I reasoned that Palm Springs might be the place to write them. I remembered my deal with the Universe---nice place to live and adequate income. Hmmmm. The only thing I forgot to consult was my guidance.

THE BED AND BREAKFAST ON STEROIDS

*Time is a fabrication within this plane of existence, and it
simply cannot connect in the multiple planes of existence in
which you actually function, and therefore, it is very difficult
for you to hold on to time because it is not
part of what you truly experience.*

–The Immortal Now

On my way to Palm Springs, I decided to take a circuitous route and see my sister, Bonny, in Bozeman, Montana. I stopped in Coeur d'Alene, Idaho, by the water near a park in the downtown area and saw a beautiful white house. It would have made a perfect bed and breakfast.

"Dummy, now you do not have the economic base to qualify for such a house, even with the money from the sale of the Alaska house." Sigh!

Then I had the urge to do the writing. What? It said to use the white light meditation and think of having a bed and breakfast, which I did.

I continued on to Bozeman, had a great visit with Bonny, and started toward Livingston, Montana, when an almost audible voice said, "Go to the Grabow Hotel and tell them that if they ever to wish to sell it, your family would like to buy it back." So I pulled off I-90 and drove into Livingston.

My grandfather on my father's side, William Grabow, born in Germany in 1850, had come to Livingston shortly after the railroad arrived in 1884. He married my beloved grandmother in 1892. Livingston was the original entrance to Yellowstone and was accommodating around thirty thousand visitors a year on six trains a day. Thirteen hotels were built to provide baths and housing for the new Yellowstone tourists who had just traveled over one thousand miles on the train. William Grabow had the liquor license for Park County and Yellowstone National Park and sold it to build the Grabow Hotel in 1908. Sadly, he died in the flu epidemic of 1918 along with 25 percent of Livingston's population. My six-foot grandmother, Elizabeth, ran the Grabow Hotel until 1937 when an attorney, a banker, and a politician contrived to wrest it away from her towards the end of the Great Depression. My father, Harry Grabow, was the assistant manager of the Waldorf Astoria in New York and came out to Montana to try to save the family hotel. The trip failed in its mission but had a positive outcome for all of us since, the following summer, he drove a Yellowstone Park bus and met my mother in Mammoth Hot Springs.

My parents had four children all twenty-one months apart: Harry, the oldest, then Gretchen, me, and Bonny. Elizabeth Grabow was eighty-five years old when I was born, and I adored her. She lived until I was ten, so I had very fond memories of her. Now, I was thrilled at the prospect of, at least, seeing the Grabow Hotel again.

I drove into the parking lot for the Depot Café to get a cup of coffee and listen for anyone who might have knowledge of Livingston's history. I knew which building had been the Grabow. It had been an elegant forty-unit hotel where people like John D. Rockefeller stayed on their way to Yellowstone.

An older man stood out. His name was Warren, and we became fast friends. I asked him if he knew anything about the Grabow Hotel, and he said he thought the building was for sale. "Do you know where I might find out about it?"

"Yes, I think a woman at the Empire Bank may know," he replied, and he gave me directions to where I might find her.

When I spoke with her, she said that, indeed, it was for sale and gave me the name of the realtor with the listing. I went right to him, and he said, "I'm sorry. We do not have any Grabow Hotel."

"The building kitty-corner from here," I replied.

"Oh, that is the Swandal Building."

"Oh no, that is not the Swandal Building. It is the Grabow Hotel," I emphasized.

He showed me the building. It had been sorely neglected, but the bones were amazing: a grand staircase to the three floors, with hallways made of all bird's-eye maple, high ceilings, and oak floors in each unit. It had fifteen apartments and three grand commercial spaces with thirteen-foot ceilings on the first floor. There was extensive water damage, and it looked like serious work to renovate it, but something told me that I was meant to do this.

I fell in love on the spot.

I went out to the cemetery in Livingston where most of my family was buried, including my dad, and I said to their graves, "If I am supposed to have this, please help me, and if I am not supposed to have it, please stop me!"

The real estate expertise of my sister, Bonny, enabled me to buy it on a contract for deed. The McArthurs helped me initially, and I paid them back. I had the bed and breakfast I had asked the Universe for, only bigger, more beautiful, with eighteen units, and a symbolic healing of an ancient trauma for my family. In addition, with great measures of ongoing TLC, the building provided for the stable home and income I needed in my discussions with myself and the Universe to pursue the third and fourth books I was to do. *Passage from Fear* said that when you use the white light meditation, our greater self sets up the situation in which we grow spiritually, and we then walk into whatever we ask for. I believe that.

WE REPUBLISH
PASSAGE FROM FEAR
AND PUBLISH
PASSAGE FROM KARMA

It is very easy for you, for example, to look at a scene and
then return rather instantly within a time frame. But,
what happens within that time frame is that you
travel within your own being. That is timeless.

–*The Immortal Now*

I had the bed and breakfast and everything I needed. Rob returned from Germany and spent his senior year at Park High in Livingston. Chris had moved back to the Grabow from Boston. And then Rob, after graduating from high school, was off to Gonzaga University. Right away, he began making a name for himself.

Rob graduated magna cum laude from Gonzaga and became a spokesperson for young voters. Within a year he, with his co-author, Dean Robbins, also from Gonzaga, appeared on C-Span Book TV in 2005 for an hour discussing their new book, *What We Think: Young Voters Speak Out.*

Rob and Dean appeared on MSNBC, CNN, and national and local programs everywhere to promote their book. Rob showed all signs of what has been called the Indigo generation. The writing said that he was part of the preparation for the events thirty years from the beginning of the books. Later it dawned on me that it was talking about 2012!

In addition, the writing said that Rob was also part of humanity preparing for, and adjusting to, the next one hundred years, which was referred to in the very first writing session for *Passage from Fear*.

I hired a friend, Dan, to edit *Passage from Fear*, and we republished it along with *Passage from Karma* through a small publishing house owned by my friend Sheryn. Dan's wife, a professional artist, designed the covers with symbols that been used by the writing during the generation of the books—eight circles and eight infinity signs. When these symbols appeared in the writing, I learned that they were associated with an upcoming time of peace for me that was welcomed with open arms. Dan also created a web site for the books. It was a milestone to see the books in print and have information regarding them on the Internet.

SECTION FOUR

THE IMMORTAL NOW

THE THIRD BOOK,
THE IMMORTAL NOW,
COMES INTO BEING

It is difficult for you to understand the nature of cosmic time,
of cosmic growth, of cosmic awareness. It is beyond your
greatest imagination at this time, but it is very real.

–*The Immortal Now*

I had the Grabow Hotel for about two years when the books began to re-emerge. One day, a lovely woman and her young friend rented an apartment at the Grabow. She had been led to Livingston through prayer and loved the place. We had a lively discussion and shared the books at length.

With Chris in Livingston helping with the building, I was able to take trips to Arizona to see my dear friend, Charlotte McArthur, as often as I could. Bruce, sadly, had passed on a few years earlier. It had been twenty years since the books, *Passage from Fear* and *Passage from Karma*, had written themselves with the support from the McArthurs. As far as I was concerned, the McArthur family was my own as well, and I loved them.

As mentioned before, Bruce had published his book on the Universal Laws of Cause and Effect, *Your Life: Why It Is the Way It Is and What You Can Do About It*. It explained our role in creating most of our experience through our thoughts, feelings, beliefs, and actions. He and David McArthur had also been studying the process of transformation and what they came to know as the "Intelligent Heart." Some people transformed their lives and often debilitating situations into ones that were meaningful and empowering. The engine for that transformation, they learned, was the experience of love in that Intelligent Heart.

Bruce and David learned of Doc Lew Childre and his work at the Institute of HeartMath in Boulder Creek, California. Childre was bringing together scientific discoveries about our intelligent heart and developing technologies people could use to access its profound wisdom and truth quickly. Charlotte told me that HeartMath had done studies that proved that the heart was forty to fifty times more powerful than our head. Finally, science was beginning to understand my near-death experience and the transformative power of the heart.

Bruce and David worked with Childre and HeartMath for several years. David McArthur had left the ministry for his time with HeartMath, serving on their staff plus traveling around the country and giving workshops. The awareness of the wisdom in our intelligent hearts with the tools that HeartMath provided to help people access that wisdom and energy was growing with appearances on television shows like *The View*.

At the time of Bruce's death, he and David were writing a book called *The Intelligent Heart*, which combined their understanding of Cayce's Laws of Transformation with the tools of HeartMath.

On one of my trips to see Charlotte in Missoula, Montana, she showed me material and pictures of David's involvement with HeartMath and his now-published book, *The Intelligent Heart*. As any mother would be, she was proud of her son's commitment to the well-being of others.

During the course of our conversation, the topic turned to the nature of forgiveness. Charlotte turned to me and said that she was going to tell me about something she had not felt free to discuss until then.

When Charlotte began her narrative, I realized the horror and depth of the struggle for David and his parents while we were in Jackson. They were so very kind to me, my baby, and sons, but they were working through a hell of their own and could say nothing about it. David had kept it a secret for years and did not speak publicly of it until he was ready. In his book, *The Intelligent Heart*, David at last told his story.

Charlotte told me that a few years before I arrived in Jackson, David was a law student with a beautiful wife, Kathy, and a year-old baby. They had taken a young man into their home to help him. One day, David came home from work and the baby was in the crib. The young man and David's wife were gone. What happened to Kathy was unspeakable. The young man had murdered David's wife. The remarkable part of the story was that when David made the decision to forgive, the McArthurs as a family made the decision to forgive as well. No wonder Bruce had been so adamant about my forgiving Robert!

According to Charlotte, David had spent a great deal of time using his legal connections keeping the young man out of traditional prisons and into mental institutions. The young man eventually escaped from the mental institution and died in a drowning in the Salmon River. Several years later, David left the practice of law and became a Unity minister. He remarried and had two more children with his wonderful wife. David always said that his forgiveness of the young man was his decision to stay on the higher planes of consciousness for the sake of his daughter and, finally, for himself.

I just could not get over the fact that they had never told me what they were going through. Maybe I could have been more supportive in some way had I known. It was unbelievable to me that anyone would ever want to hurt these loving people. Even more remarkable was that they would so openly and almost desperately choose to forgive. Mine had been a roundabout forgiveness of Robert at Bruce's urging. Charlotte comforted me and told me that, in a sense, I was support to them. They could see more clearly the necessity of their consistent stand on forgiveness because they were helping me.

She said they loved the books that were being generated at the time, *Passage from Fear* and *Passage from Karma*. The books were articulating what they already knew at some level. I believe that I had been the recipient of the spiritual strength the McArthurs had gained when they had made the choices to move on and forgive from their hearts. When we completed *Passage from Karma*, David publicly endorsed the book because of his experience and what the book had to say about the nature of love. They all loved the work and spent the better part of their adulthood being moral support for me as I remained obedient to the guidance I received for half of a lifetime.

Later, when Rosie Porter and I were gallivanting around the country, we stopped by to see Charlotte who had moved to Flagstaff, Arizona, to be closer to her son, Thomas. When we arrived, the three of us decided to do a session. Much to our surprise, the session said that it was time to start the third book on alternative realities and that Christine, the woman at the Grabow, and Charlotte would help with it as Barbara McCormick had done twenty years earlier. It was exciting. The writing said specifically that the next book would be entitled *The Immortal Now: The Ascension and the Nature of the Present Time*. When Rosie and I returned from the Southwest and told Christine the good news, she was thrilled.

Christine and her friend, Matthew, had been married at the Grabow. The building had been remodeled by then and showed the beauty that my grandparents had originally created. It had the last grand staircase in the city, and on her wedding day, Christine came down the stairs decorated with turquoise, peach, soft green ribbons, and peach-colored roses to meet her husband-to-be, Matthew, on the landing. They exchanged their vows and turned to greet the audience of about forty friends in the lobby. Chris was Matthew's best man. She and Matthew glowed with the love they felt for each other, and everything blended into a collage of happiness, celebration, love, and hope for the kind of support possible with two people who love each other.

Christine spent a good part of her day praying for others. Like other natural healers, she felt the malady as people came to see her for prayer. At one point when Martha was close to dying of pancreatitis, she flew down from Alaska with her daughter to be with Christine as she prayed for Martha's healing.

When Martha arrived, the doctors had given her little hope of survival, and she could hardly make it up the stairs. Martha stayed with me since Christine and I lived on the second floor. Three days later, Martha was significantly better, and she walked down those same stairs with ease, ready to return to Alaska and keep up with her grandchildren for several years to come.

So here I was, bargain kept. In addition to having a steady income, the wonderful bed and breakfast on steroids, and my children taken care of, the people around me who were to help with the books, according to the writing, were ready as well.

My near-death experience and my work for the earlier books had been teaching me that what I had been taught as truth from the various churches I had attended turned out not to be true after all, at least not for me.

I could hardly wait to start on *The Immortal Now*.

THE SESSIONS BEGIN

*[The scientific community] has explored what it calls
the physical universe and physics and chemistry and
mathematics and all areas but the power of love. It has
sought nuclear energy and any form of energy it could find,
but ignored the greatest and only power that exists.*

−*The Immortal Now*

I showed Christine how to do the sessions, and she was quick
to catch on. The only problem was finding the time in our
lives to get together. Generally, we would meet, much as Barbara and I had, in one of our apartments. The sessions were
similar to those that generated the first two books. I would use
the white light meditation and lie down, covered with a small
blanket, and the books would dictate themselves. As had happened with the previous books, before the text began, the session said how many pages and chapters it would have, along
with the entire design of the book. It would have twelve chapters, the writing said, and would be about 160 pages long with
three sections.

Once it let us know the details of the book, it went right
to work. It started with the longest chapter on peace. The first
segment of the book dealt with the Middle East as well as the
concept of peace within the individual:

*When the world longs for peace, it truly longs for it within
each individual. It is a spiritual goal, not a group goal, so
world peace is not possible. What is possible is individual
peace, and the world reflects that individual peace... .*

The goal is peace within the individual. Whatever contributes to that peace contributes to the world situation.

To say the least, the sessions were exciting to Christine and me as they unfolded.

The night after the session, I would transcribe it and send the day's work to a small circle of friends, including those who had been supportive of the work all along: David and Charlotte McArthur, Rosie Porter, my sons, and others who had expressed an interest in the books.

Parallel to the sessions dictating *The Immortal Now*, we did guidance sessions to help Christine and me on what to do as we worked on the book. The guidance sessions were almost as fascinating as *The Immortal Now*, but in an entirely different way. They seemed to be focused more on helping us understand the global events that were occurring around all of us. The book said,

Imagine that the world reaches a point where all it feels is love. Imagine the anger, the revenge, the distrust—all of those things—simply vanishing. It is not a loss as the traditional religions have characterized it. It is freedom beyond your imagination. It is ready for this remarkable transformation.

Early on, the book dealt with symbology—what we often think is true, like words and images, are merely symbols of something that is real.

There is much joy in the nature of who you are. You deal in symbols here on this plane of existence. Words, images, feelings about images, and objects are symbols. But God within a theological base is still symbology. It is a time in which you separate symbology from reality.

A couple of friends of mine who were reading the sessions after the day's work said that they had never thought of this experience as being made up largely as symbols.

The Immortal Now used the image of the relationship with a tree:

> *To know the reality of the tree is to see beyond symbol. There is spirit within the tree. There is life within the tree. There is soul within the tree. As you move to higher planes of consciousness within the present time, you see the other elements of the tree. It is by glimpse. The only place in which you do not deal in symbology is within love.... . When you are at one with the tree and love the tree, you are present with the tree. When you remember the tree and the symbol of the tree, you are no longer in the present with the tree.*

I had loved trees all of my life and could understand this illustration. I could feel the difference. I remember my first trip out of Montana at six years of age where one of our stops was the redwood forests of northern California. I felt love with complete abandon. Its location was within me, and I could almost hear it in the beat of my heart. At the moment I looked at one of those giant trees with the light pouring through it, the only thoughts I had were appreciation and love. I cried then, I loved them so much. Like the ancient, patient Buddha, they were spiritual giants silently growing where they were planted and filled with life in its stillest form. I saw a postcard that said, "Sink down, oh traveler, on your knees. God stands before you with these trees." My parents bought me that postcard, and I cherished it.

It was wonderful that the dictation of the third book came in segments. After transcribing a session, I'd send it back to

Christine, and we would have a chance to visit with each other before the next one. We got together as often as our lives would allow.

The guidance sessions were saying:

> As 'the veil' lifts, it means that symbolism becomes less and less important. The connection with the tree itself becomes more and more important, until all that exists is the connection with the tree itself and the painting on the mirror, or the tree, is not important.

The Immortal Now was saying things like:

> The prayer that has been given is like an arrow piercing through the belief system of the world. It is breaking the barrier of the human belief system.

One time, we drove from Livingston up into Yellowstone to do a session on *The Immortal Now*. The meadows and valleys of Yellowstone have always been my havens: the Lamar Valley with its wolves, elk, and buffalo; the Hayden Valley, a stop for migratory birds and wildlife; and a small meadow just outside of Mammoth Hot Springs near the Gibbon Falls that we chose as a spot for our sessions. I went into the white light meditation, and Christine ran the tape recorder. The sessions were always fascinating, though we both knew that they did, in fact, take energy.

GUIDANCE INCLUDES CHARLOTTE AND ARIZONA

You will see that the world does not see the vision of what is coming. It cannot visualize the nature of the ascension. It is beyond any image that has been created within the human consciousness.

–The Immortal Now

The writing said that I needed to go to Arizona and work with Charlotte McArthur for part of the book. I flew down to Phoenix on my way to Munds Park outside of Flagstaff. Thomas picked me up at the airport and took me back to their new home which he and his bride-to-be, Susan, shared with Charlotte. Thomas and Susan had chosen the house specifically for Charlotte, who was ninety years young, and for Thomas's work as a filmmaker.

The last time I had seen Charlotte was at a beautiful retirement home in Flagstaff where we were told that the third book would begin. At the time, Rosie and I sensed that Charlotte was lonely, though she never let on. Thomas and Susan, who were living in Sedona at the time, had sensed it as well. They chose Munds Park since it was out of the heat, which Charlotte could not tolerate.

It was wonderful to see Thomas and Susan again, and they helped Charlotte and me in any way they could for the two weeks I spent there. Susan was a wonderful cook and went out of her way to make sure that everyone ate well. Charlotte and I did the sessions in her apartment, which was part of the large house.

As you walked into her new home, you could sense Charlotte in every way. First, its brilliant white couch and needlepoint chairs were impeccably clean. Everything about Charlotte had been immaculate. I always felt that she was clear in her thoughts, her actions, and her love for everything and everyone. A huge original painting of a mountain man in the Teton Mountains filled the wall, and everywhere were pictures of her husband, her children, her grandchildren, and now her great-grandchildren. We were surrounded with love.

Charlotte did as Barbara and Christine had. She was moral support and ran the tape recorder.

As always, we worked as long as our energy would allow us. *The Immortal Now* was becoming even more interesting. I sensed that it would be a bear to transcribe. Charlotte had always been fascinated by earth changes that were predicted for 2012. Would an asteroid actually hit the earth on December 20 of that year? There were a lot of books being written about the end of the world. The man in Seattle who Bruce and Charlotte had wanted me to meet to learn how to do "voice communication" predicted violent earth changes in his writings. Charlotte was curious. One of the chapters we worked on was on earth changes. It said,

> *In order to understand earth changes, one must understand the earth. One must understand the relationship of all life and understand the nature of the characteristics of the earth. If one were to describe the earth, one would describe it as a ball of life, a focus of life, a concentration of life, a place of life with myriad forms of life expressing itself. One would not describe it as life-less. One would equate life with the earth.*

Then the session went on to talk briefly about what it calls the World of Fear, and the fear that some scientists have that the earth is the only place where life exists. The session said,

The greatest shift that is taking place within this paradigm is that they [the scientists] are discovering life within, and once that discovery is made, then perception of life on earth will change.

It went on to say,

The reality of life is the nature of love, is the nature of truth, is the nature of spirit that exists. That is all that exists, truly, so that the fear-based thought, like the fog that vanishes, simply vanishes. Does that alter the earth? Does that alter life? Does that alter anything? No, it does not. It only vanishes, and what remains is what always existed, what has always been the nature of being.

The chapter on earth changes spoke of the ascension, the topic of so many of those books predicting the end of the world in 2012.

The Christians believe that the world will be destroyed, but how can you destroy something that is not real? The reality of existence is within the moment, within the Presence, within the present time. You cannot destroy something within the present time.

Charlotte smiled when we came out of the session.

"I knew that what the session said exists," she said, "but was not sure how. There is some level at which I understand it, and Patricia, it is what I needed to hear." She looked so filled with peace. Working on the book was enlarging for her as well, she said, because it answered some of her own questions.

When the two weeks were over, I flew back to Livingston. It was difficult to leave Charlotte this time. I remember her frail hug and kiss on the cheek like my experience of holding my baby for the first time. To say that I, and anyone who knew Charlotte McArthur, loved her is simply an understatement. Moving within ten feet of her, anyone felt a waft of pure love enveloping him or her, like a flower-laden spring breeze. It was freeing just to be near her. Her eyes still sparkled like a young child, and her ready, humble laugh was infectious. I had been given the privilege of knowing one of the greatest gifts in my life as a simple friend.

In Charlotte was everything I loved: kindness, unconditional love for everyone and everything, and an intelligent, soul-filled perspective on truth itself. I knew we would not be given the privilege of having her with us for much longer. That was the next to the last time I saw Charlotte. That hug and kiss on the cheek still warms my heart.

The Immortal Now: The Ascension and the Nature of the Present Time was published before I left for Charlotte's memorial service. It was held at a beautiful chapel in Munds Park, which was enveloped by tall Ponderosa pines and the rich smell of new flowers. Loving friends came from everywhere, including people like the kind and gentle Charles Thomas Cayce, Edgar Cayce's grandson. David conducted the service. At the end of the service, he had difficulty talking of Charlotte's support for him through the period involving his wife's murder. It was as though she were there comforting us all.

The Immortal Now was given to many attending the service. It was a time of celebration, though, with the gathering of her three children, David, Thomas, and Sue, her grandchildren, and her great grandchildren, as well as her enormous extended family, including Rosie and me. We shared stories and memories and watched as her great-grandchildren spoke as mature adults about their beloved Grandmother Charlotte.

THE GUIDANCE SESSIONS

In many ways, the story is the opening of that door of the small room and allowing the light of the heart to enter, and as that occurred, then the healing took place for Patricia. Much of the assistance in opening the door was through what the book calls soul mates because they are of the same heart, of the same awareness, of the same understanding, of the same, almost physiology.

−Guidance Session, January 18, 2012

The third book, *The Immortal Now,* was completed, and many of those who had helped me were gone. A huge chasm remained in the hearts of those of us who loved them. But life, as it must, was continuing.

People who heard me share my near-death experience and the remarkable insights I gained from the writings kept encouraging me to write my story. At the same time, the guidance sessions were providing Christine, me, and others with important understandings about what was going on globally at this time, especially about what was happening politically throughout the world.

My sons, each in his own way, were involved in the world. They saw themselves as members of the world community with a responsibility to contribute to it. While they were growing up, it was important to me and to Walter, who was an international correspondent by then, that our children understand they were citizens of the world. Chris and Tim were able to live across the planet when they stayed with Walter and had exposure to the

Middle East and Europe. They traveled extensively wherever he was working.

Chris and Tim were making significant contributions in their respective fields, but being the private persons that they are, they preferred staying out of the public eye.

Rob had a curiosity about the world even when we lived in bush Alaska. He said as a young child that he wanted to live across the planet. Having five exchange students live with us while he was growing up only furthered that interest. Rob was also very focused on his generation globally—what they thought about politics and God and the impact he believed they would have on political arenas. He was able to illustrate who they were with stories, humor, and complete abandon and called them "the greatest generation" during his talk on C-Span Book Notes about the impact of young voters.

Interestingly, the guidance sessions called Rob's generation the "transformative generation" and said that they were willing to "risk everything, globally, to relinquish systems of fear." The writing said, "Rob was able to articulate much of what is happening for those who have come here to make this transition." Little did I know that with another presidential election looming, Rob was beginning to write his second book, *Voting with Our Pants Down: Why 44 Million Young Voters Have the Power to Start the World Over Again.*

Voting with Our Pants Down came out too late in the elections cycle to catch on fire, but it remains a clear, fun-loving story, filled with well-written characterizations of his peers and their involvement in the politics.

Recently, as I watched the birthing of the Arab Spring on television, I was seeing the power of this young transformative generation Rob had been discussing in his books. He had predicted the uprisings of the Arab Spring a year earlier in an essay he wrote for admission into graduate school. These young people believed that change was possible. Rather than just wanting to overthrow a political system, they wanted freedom and a better life for the people in their countries. Their energy became a magnet pulling women and men and fathers with young babies who had been silenced out onto the streets to join them, mobilizing entire countries of individuals and then the world into a force that confronted fear in the face.

Through their vision and action, they created the change they wanted to see. One of the guidance sessions said:

> *It is very important to understand that at this point because the events in the Middle East will allow you to see that each being is connected to every other being and, symbolically, the Internet is what is connecting, but it is actually what is occurring spiritually within the individual. It looks like there is a revolution. It looks like the Internet and social media, but what it is, is the interconnectedness of all life including other forms of life as well. It is one. There is nothing else. It is so important at this point to understand that what is emerging is the understanding of what is within the book [The Immortal Now].*

I remember thinking that this was almost like puberty. The transformation happening with puberty occurs without our being totally aware of it. In my pre-teen years, I had no idea that my body would soon be going through changes in order to prepare me for adulthood in which I would do what I must, allow the next generation to come through me. The interesting thing about puberty is that all of humanity and all of life goes through it. It is a flow within the present.

The guidance sessions said there is more love in individual lives now, which is creating what David McArthur calls, a "tsunami of love." The guidance said that we are almost oblivious to what is going on beneath us as we are surfing on the top of that massive wave. We do not recognize the depth of the love we are all experiencing as we are being released from the grip of the world paradigm of fear into one of love.

One of the guidance sessions said,

> *The healing is occurring even though it doesn't look like it is occurring within the forms of life on this planet—the awareness of global warming, the awareness of connectedness, the Internet—all of the things that are symptomatic out there are occurring within the individual.*

The writings said that truth is within the individual, within the heart, not in an external reality or belief system. David McArthur said that after his wife was killed and he began his training as a Unity minister, he could not even force himself to read a generalized, theoretical treatise—quite a feat for a former attorney. Instead, all he could read were individual stories because that was where the truth resided.

The guidance had said that the books I was told to do were for thirty years beyond my near-death experience: the year 2012 and beyond. It was not as a huge mega-movement but as an individual experience. The guidance sessions said that 2012 was never meant to be an event but, rather, a very powerful concept.

> *You will see that what is happening around you is not happening as much as what is happening within you— within your own consciousness, within your own paradigm, within your view of the world, so that the things that are coming up for you to face are things within your own consciousness. That is happening universally.*

So we are in this thing together—as individuals. We are at one with the present in which, as the guidance said,

It is not outside you individually. It is within you, so that when you confront those things that are fearful or of concern or old ambitions or are old romances or are old paradigms that you have faced before and not resolved on a very grand scale—you are resolving them.

EPILOGUE

Looking back at my life with all of the challenges, all of the fears and the mistakes I made born out of those fears—and I made some big ones—I realize that my life has been, and is, perfect for the work I was to do. Being born a seeker who was trying to find truth in different theologies and belief systems, and who just wanted to know the truth and look it straight in the eye laid the foundation for what I was to experience when I died.

I faced death and found that I was fully alive, just as conscious as I am now when I am in a deep conversation with a friend, feeling a love to the millionth power I can barely describe and filled with a crystalline truth that continues to guide me throughout my life. All I am and all anyone is, is life and love to the millionth power, whether we are on this plane of existence or not. Consciousness, I realized, rests within my heart, not in my body and not in my intellect. It continues on, whether my physical body dies or not. I have experienced that.

The freedom from that fear of death—one of life's greatest and most limiting fears—has been liberating for me beyond description. It has also served me well. My parents, who were children of Montana pioneers, were people true to their word. They taught me that I had a responsibility to make a contribution to my community and humanity. I have been known to speak my truth boldly and unconsciously fight for change I believed in, whether it was filing the EEOC complaint for sexual harassment, confronting the players of financial mismanagement during my mistaken venture as a city commissioner, or sharing my journey with you now as a near-death survivor.

The consequent revelations forced me to re-evaluate everything I thought I knew about death, life, and where truth and power reside. I would feel the risk and remember what Dannion Brinkley, a well-known near-death survivor, said: "What are they going to do. Kill me? I've already died." And with a chuckle, the fear would melt away, and I could act upon what I knew I must do.

My marriage to Walter brought into my life and to this world, two amazing sons who are brilliant, ethical to the core, and committed to bettering humanity and the earth through their lives and business ventures. Recently, while writing this book, my sons and I talked for the first time about the accident and the impact of that experience on their lives. It is one of those horrific experiences you often cannot speak your truth about without the passage of a lot of time.

"It's amazing," Tim said, "that I didn't turn to drugs." It is true. Had it not been for his sharp mind and remarkable intellectual curiosity, his deep connection to his brothers and family who loved him, and his talent and passion for skiing that absorbed him completely, we might very well have lost him to drugs as a way of dealing with his own uncertainty and pain.

Had I not died in that horrific car crash in London and then been pulled back to life to care for my sons, I would not have experienced my truth and looked it squarely in the eye. The love, the truth, the power I was seeking, which I called God, was the love to the millionth power I experienced when

I died. That love, that truth, that wisdom, and that power rest within the heart.

That One Power of love within our hearts comes through us in many different forms, as a river flowing down a mountain as many streams is also one with the ocean. That Power within each one of us in our hearts, as we are pulled together, can create amazing changes in the world. We are seeing that everywhere.

And now, for my relationship with Robert—the one I entered that left me destitute emotionally, financially, and on the brink of suicide. He was my teacher of love by adversity. If I had not lost everything and been so desperate, I would not have been open to receiving the remarkable guidance, and I certainly would not have followed it for it did not come to me in a way that my rational mind could trust. I wanted to find truth in concrete things I could see, read, and know with my intellectual, logical mind. I had to be on the brink with nothing to lose to follow that slim, silver strand of hope presented to me in the writing.

Had I not been in relationship with Robert again, with the determination to give birth to that beautiful baby in spite of my fear of raising him without a father, we would not have my amazing son, Rob. His birth, which coincided with the writing of *Passage from Fear*, was not an accident. It is as if the wisdom, the concepts—the love—in *Passage from Fear* are woven into his DNA.

All along the way, that Power, that Source that was guiding me so completely, gave me the pieces of concrete proof I needed to keep going, to keep trusting: finding the man at the Silver Dollar Bar who ended up renting me his beautiful log house on the stream in Wilson; the jobs, even those I obtained through Robert, that helped me support my family; being guided to a

Cayce meeting I knew nothing about only to connect with the soul mates of Barbara McCormick and then Bruce and Charlotte McArthur and their children, David, Thomas, and Sue. They understood my work completely and the way it needed to come through me, though I could not even comprehend at the time.

The guidance to soul mates continued with Rosie Porter, my chosen sister who gets the concepts and understandings of this work. She has been instrumental in the writing and publishing of the books, including this one when she sat at my house for two weeks putting me through a relentless schedule of twenty-minute writes to finish getting this story of my journey out while she edited the manuscript and put together ideas for the cover. To say that we were exhausted at the end and needed to recover for weeks is an understatement.

To have Christine and her soon-to-be husband cross my path at the Grabow was nothing short of miraculous, though I have come to expect such things from the guidance. Her work as a prayer warrior and healer, as well as providing the supportive environment and taping of the sessions for *The Immortal Now* after Barbara's passing, was essential.

What I have learned from looking back is that salvation did not come from where I thought it would—by being a good, moral person seeking truth and believing in a version of God that would eventually save me when I got to heaven. It did not come from having a husband and being a loving wife with sons in a normal, nuclear family. It happened by tuning into my heart, to that love to the millionth power I experienced when I died, through my white light meditations, the guidance sessions, and my writings. I was led to extraordinary people who were so filled with that love and compassion to the millionth power in their own hearts. They cared enough to literally save me. In turn, I have been able to help others.

For me, it is not religion in any form. It supersedes that. Eventually, I believe that love to the millionth power will be proved to be the nature of reality. Love within is our very substance that resides in the heart, in all life, without time, and it is real. As with quantum physics, I believe that seekers of the truth in the scientific community will eventually prove what the eight-plus million near-death survivors have learned. Ultimately, for me, it is no longer life, then death, then heaven—it is now. It is not sinner/saint, it is love beyond our wildest imagination, but experienced every day. The soul mates, the guidance, the books, the meditation were my strength as they are for all individuals—in whatever form it takes. It is what is real in our lives.

Gratitude for all of it overwhelms me at times. The hope is to continue to be obedient to the guidance and also helpful to others. At this important juncture in all of our lives as predicted thirty years ago, I believe that life and love and the solutions needed for beyond 2012 exist within the individual, within the now, and are accessible by tuning into the heart. My experience has been that you walk into the solutions your Larger Being has created for you when you use something like the white light meditation or prayer. I believe we are beings of love creating solutions.

The guidance sessions have been extraordinarily accurate for guiding me along this journey. They provide powerful and easy-to-understand messages designed to help us make sense out of the major transformations people, the earth, and all life are going through at this time. I have included some of the recent guidance sessions in Appendix 2, Parts of Guidance Sessions, that you might find helpful. I will also be sharing more on our website, www.TheImmortalNow.com, as the guidance sessions continue. I invite you to join us there as we continue our journeys.

> *Those who have had near-death experiences have understood this because, at that point, they visited their own being. They visited the life of the Life. They visited the love of the Love.*
>
> *They visited the truth of the Truth and then emerged as individuals who understood that larger being.*
>
> *That Larger Being is the substance of life. It is the substance of all truth. It is the background of all mathematics.*
>
> *It is the substance sound of all music. It is the beauty of all art. It is the laughter of a child ...*
>
> −*The Immortal Now*

ACKNOWLEDGMENTS

B ecause there is so much to acknowledge in my life, it took *Love to the Millionth Power*, an entire book, to do so. This book recognizes all of those who meant so much in the creation of the story, especially my sons, whose lives gave my life meaning. It has been an entire lifetime of meeting those who deserve acknowledgment. We are one, and I know that for sure. My appreciation of those in this book and beyond is truly without limit. There are several people, however, who are not mentioned in the book. I met them after *The Immortal Now* was finished.

I was still following the guidance, and it told me go to the church where my friend, David McArthur, was a minister, and I would meet the tech person who would help me with the task of getting the books out to the world with social media. I obediently drove twelve hundred miles from Montana in my small RV to California, and I kept thinking to myself, *What AM I doing? The tech persons involved in David's church have busy lives and will not have time to do all that has to be done in the social media.*

By the time I arrived in California, I was convinced that this was the time that the guidance would be wrong and I would have to go back the twelve hundred miles I had just driven.

The nearest RV park was seventeen miles south of where David and his family lived. A wonderful woman, Cheryl McLaughlin, checked me in as a camp host. We struck up a conversation, and it turns out that getting books out across the planet through social media was her specialty. We are still working together. She has been my tough-minded editor, confidante, social-media guru, and friend.

While all of that was going on, back at the Grabow, my friend whom I left managing the building called me. I had mentioned to her an acquaintance, Debbie Sullivan, and said that if she needed a place to stay at any point that I had a spare bedroom. She definitely needed a place, and a Montana winter was closing in. My friend said the problem was that Debbie had three dogs, one of which was a 130-pound Rottweiler! The upshot was that Debbie was also a tech, social-media whiz. I ended up trading space for her and her dogs in the terrazzo-floored, daylight basement in the building for work on Twitter and everything else that her expanding consciousness would allow. I have been working with Debbie ever since.

In addition, I would like to acknowledge Sheryn Hara of Book Publisher's Network. I met Sheryn a couple of decades ago when she was giving a talk about publishing books. She has been a friend ever since and a help in every aspect of book publishing as the books emerged. She has a remarkable team of professionals she works with: Julie Scandora, Marcia Breece, Stephanie Martindale, and Laura Zugzda.

Most of all, I wish to acknowledge whatever Wisdom that has never left me, no matter how myopic my decisions became or how limited the scope of my own thought was. There really are no words for what that Presence is, but it is always there, and my heart sings whenever I think of it. Gratitude is such a small word in light of its scope.

Appendix 1
White Light Meditation

Here is an explanation of how to use the white light meditation from the chapter, "The White Light," in *Passage from Fear*, page 219.

> *When you use the White Light, you will lie down and envision a brilliant white light; do not think about breathing or about your surroundings or about your troubles, only envision light. At the last moment before you are lifted, you can think about your goal, but you will understand that you can only use the White Light for good, either for yourself or others.*

It has been my experience that it is simple. People seem to want more from it than it actually involves. They expect to see a light. Sometimes you do not. They expect to have a physical experience, and that is not the nature of it. It is almost like just turning towards the light.

My experience is that when the writing talks about envisioning a goal, it can be truly whatever you wish, and it will never create harm.

The Immortal Now shares the following about the white light meditation.

> *It is a process in which you simply envision light. You do not need to see the light. You do not need to experience the light. You just intend the light, and it is like opening a window towards it. It allows the individual to see his or*

her path, even though the words do not come to describe the path.

APPENDIX 2
PARTS OF GUIDANCE SESSIONS

Following are excerpts from some of the guidance sessions that you might find helpful. Some of the sessions were simply personal. We are presenting them from the more recent January 25, 2013 session to the past session on January 23, 2009. You might find it intriguing to read them from the past to the present. We will be sharing more from the guidance sessions on the website at www.TheImmortalNow.com as they occur, as well as on Twitter. We invite you to join us on the journey.

January 25, 2013

> *You will see that there is so very much for you to under-*
> *stand now that you have completed what is called "2012."*
> *When one really understands what the nature of the*
> *present time is, one understands that those are simply*
> *numbers, at random, essentially. What happens is the*
> *depth, the breadth, the height, the might, the majesty of*
> *love that permeates all things and permeates whatever*
> *fears are created by what is called "consciousness," but it*
> *is not consciousness. It is the filter of what is called the*
> *brain, but it is not the brain. It is the filter of what the*
> *writing calls the World of Fear.*

That consciousness, that filter, that fear, is a simple veil. It has been referred to biblically as a veil, but it is not a physical veil. It is ephemeral. There is no substance to it.

It is important to understand what you call 2013 is, essentially, the work within The Immortal Now beginning to permeate thought. It is not because of the efforts of a given body or series of bodies, or series of individuals. It is like the truth. It exists, and so it permeates thought as genuine existence. It is what exists. It is what gives substance to life. It is real—therefore, it is continuous to the cosmos.

Patricia will go back to California and begin to more and more often appear with recordings, because when she is recording, this substance is visible. It looks as if she is talking, and it looks as if what she is saying is coming through and makes sense to the listener. But, there is a visibility [in the mind's eye] like when one adds 2 + 2 = 4—you actually do not see the numbers; you see concepts within your consciousness and, therefore, you can work with them. It is not a physical thing. It has not substance, per se, but it is all substance.

It is a time of great joy—a time of great exploration. It is like the time of Christopher Columbus in terms of finding a new world. What is happening is finding a new world. It is beginning to develop very quickly. The year 2013 is a time of solidifying all that has been done with the books. It was important that all books be completed by 2012. Now it is time to anchor the work.

October 25, 2012

You will see that the path that Patricia has chosen is one in which she consolidates that which she believes with what she understands. There is a difference. What she believes is that it is necessary for her to be in Livingston caring for the source of financial support, as well as caring for those who do not understand yet that the paradigm shift already has occurred. It is like being a mother with children who do not understand yet that everything that they are doing is going to be okay. She, to some degree, is playing that role to those around her to let them feel comfort with the shift that has occurred within consciousness.

But, it is only a belief. It is not the foundation of what is occurring. The foundation of what is occurring is massive beyond imagination. It isn't just human beings upon the earth. It is consciousness. Consciousness is an entirely different concept. Consciousness involves the sun, the moon, the stars, and beyond---consciousness is what some, to some degree, would call "the Mind of God."

That shift, that understanding is what has already occurred, and those who see this and understand it in their heart rejoice in it. It is the joy, the subtle, almost indiscernible joy within the heart of those who see what has happened. Christine sees this in prayer. She understands it in prayer, and to some degree, her prayers are allowing her to help those who need help.

You will see that there is much to continue to understand, but it is by glimpse. It cannot be by anything but glimpse at this point. The books, to some degree, are a glimpse. The Immortal Now and Love to the Millionth Power allow others to look through a peephole to what has actually occurred.

It will be very easy for those like Deepak Chopra and Louise Hay, and those Patricia is approaching to read The Immortal Now. They will enjoy the story, but they are ready for the concepts contained within the books.

The foundation, the love, the expansion, the joy, the peace that Christine feels does not have to be articulated in one form or the other because it has not form. Its beauty is that it is beauty. Beauty can take on form, but it exists as beauty first and always so that it is recognizable as beauty, but it has no specific form that exists more than another form that is also beautiful. It is a very important idea for Christine to understand, that within her is beauty. It exists. It is within her heart and expands from that vortex.

It is still a belief to assume what Patricia calls "life/death heaven and sinner/saint." It is a belief. The way is within. The truth is within. The love is within. There is nothing exterior. You will continue to pray and use the light, and you will see that all that you understand exists within.

August 7, 2012

You will see that there is much to understand at this point. It is important that Patricia take very good care of her body. It is a vehicle by which she is able to communicate to the world at this time, and it is part of 2012. It is a difficult concept for you to understand, but the means by which these messages come through is that body, and it needs great care right now.

The messages are an integrated whole. It is the essence of 2012. So, when the messages come through, they are actually coming through part of the past, present, and future all in one—part of the present. It is difficult for her to understand that the present exists in and of itself so that the messages are important to pull others into the present, into the nature of 2012, into the concept of 2012.

It is important that Patricia remain a messenger at this point. She does not have to disseminate the books. She has those who will help her. She has to continue to use the light, to think of abundance, to think of supply, think of allowing for that which enlarges and enlightens the entire earth.

It is difficult for you to understand the power that is part of what is considered 2012. It is like the child who thinks that when they add $2 + 2 = 4$, that is all there is. But contained within $2 + 2 = 4$ is a kind of complex mathematics that sends a rocket to the moon, that sends a vehicle to Mars. That is contained within the concept of $2 + 2 = 4$. So, when Patricia actually channels the meaning of 2012, then it actually contains within itself the entire universe of the shift within consciousness. It is occurring. It is unstoppable. It is present. So, when Patricia channels this work, it is actually an implosion of the concepts that exist within the nature of love itself.

Christine will be content and free within her environment allowing her also to move into areas of exploration that she has not truly found until now. It is an expansive, expansive process.

Patricia has received a release from the city that she has not quite been aware of, but is beginning to see. She is beginning to trust others to pick up the mantle that matters so much to her—that is the saving of the historic places in Livingston, the telling of the story. It is almost as if she built a sand castle and it is sitting on the beach. She is allowing others to enlarge it and make it even more intricate and involved, but it is important to understand that the concepts that are in the books are not the sand castles. The concepts in the books are substantial. And, it is important that she remain dedicated to the work that she is doing.

June 23, 2012

You will see that there is a presence with you at this point. There is more than you can even imagine in terms of that Presence. It is as if there is a oneness, globally. It is going on as the channeling occurs—as the books are written.

It is love right now. So, when the writing said that the books needed to become global, it did not mean that you would contact people, who would contact people, who would contact people, and then everyone would buy the books. That is not how that is working. It is as if there is a global awareness of both Love to the Millionth Power and The Immortal Now. There is that awareness right now. It exists. It is 2012. It exists in 2012.

You will go through the motion of mailing the information on the books across the planet. Therefore, there is a circular movement of the books across the entire earth, and that awareness will spread across the planet. It is important that those books get out at this time globally because what is happening is the books and other books and this awareness are global. There will be significant numbers of individuals excited about the books and buying the books now that Love to the Millionth Power is written, and it will happen, but the larger picture is the global understanding of the nature of the present time, of all of the ideas that exist within—particularly The Immortal Now.

It is important that she tell her story and let the reader interpret the content of the books. It is very important that Patricia not attempt to describe the concepts in The Immortal Now. She will simply say that there is a dynamic when you read The Immortal Now that is very personal and she cannot explain that for you. So she will have fun telling the story and affirming the guidance and affirming what happened to her, but the actual conceptual process will come between the readers and themselves. It is important that those things that open the heart are what she will gravitate toward.

March 12, 2012

You will see that there is so very much for you to understand at this point. It is necessary for Patricia to continue the writings for the story behind the books. It is very, very, very important. It has to be a completed product now. It is very urgent. That is why it seems to absorb Patricia at this point.

Awareness is not encased in time. Awareness exists—as it does with Patricia. All of this is happening in a way that is harmonious and easy for those involved. You will see that it is much like when the sun sets below the horizon. It isn't necessarily disappearing. It is simply setting to one mode of thinking and continuing on its path.

It is fear-based thought that is dissipating so rapidly. It is simply dissipating. It isn't being destroyed by the (disappearance of) the sun. The sun exists. It is a darkness that is not necessary.

It is a complex transition at this point. It is much more complex than humanity can understand. It is important that Love to the Millionth Power get out because it does point to the complexity of that transition. It is not within the realm of stereotype created by theological bases, which, of necessity, can be very, very simplified. This transition that is going on, that everyone is participating in, is a complex process that is individualized. Love to the Millionth Power allows everyone to see that it is complex. It is not simple, and it is real.

Friday, January 20, 2012

[Patricia and Rosie are putting the fourth book together, the story behind the books, *Love to the Millionth Power*. Rosie has come over from Dillon, Montana, and is editing and interjecting quotations from *The Immortal Now*.]

You will see that there is much for you to understand. At this point, it is imperative for you to finish the story behind the books and make it very clear to the reader about the nature of the present time. It is a means by which the concept can be clarified. The concept of 2012 is the concept of the transition for humanity from the fear-based paradigm into the joy and freedom of the under-standing of the present time—that there is no time, that there is the heart, that everything is within, and all of the concepts contained within the books are antithetical to much of what is taught.

It is very important that the book being written become a teacher for those concepts, much as a curriculum in a class-room is written in order to establish an idea. The means by which this reaches a global audience is prepared—is ready, in a sense, has been invented, has been created. There is an important connection that must be made between this work and HeartMath, within, at this point.

Cheryl can achieve this through the "Vook" [multimedia e-book] and it is essential to moving forward with the books. The way is like a path across the stream. It is like a means by which the individual can cross this stream in spite of the fact that the water is rushing and the belief systems are so strong and that they have been estab-lished for such a long period of time and that they are so entrenched and all of the concepts—and yet the path is there to cross the steam. It is established. It is solid. It is like rocks that have placed themselves for long enough to have stability, and that is what is happening in terms of the books reaching humanity.

There will be some resistance, but it is as if the tidal wave of love is so strong at this point that it cannot be stopped because of its existence within the heart of every single form of life upon this plane of existence right now. It has already moved in the heart. It has moved into its place. It has its stability already. You will continue the prayer and meditation and support for the nature of the present time for it truly is the foundation of everything, my beloved.

January 18, 2012, 9:00 A.M.

You will see that there is much that you discover as you continue with the work, much as Patricia discovered what could be characterized as massive rooms that she walked into as she began to use the white light meditation. She began to open doors within her own being into areas of exploration of the heart.

That is the reason for the white light meditation because the heart is so massive and so limited within this plane of existence that it is like living in a dark room and knowing that the sun is shining outside the room. It is an awareness that the sun is shining—that it is as powerful as it is, but not allowing that sunshine to be part of everyday life. It is important that the concept of the white light meditation be out there as well and that individuals can utilize it. There will be an explanation of the white light meditation as an addendum to the book itself so that other people can learn about it and practice it.

In many ways, the story is the opening of that door of the small room and allowing the light of the heart to enter, and as that occurred, then the healing took place for Patricia. Much of the assistance in opening the door was through what the book calls soul mates because they are of the same heart, of the same awareness, of the same understanding, of the same, almost, physiology.

It is a physiology of the heart, not the visual separation of identities that is experienced within what the books call the World of Fear. So it is important that the reader gets a sense of this and a sense of how wide the door began to open for Patricia from its beginning. The books will find their way, and it will be fine to the agent, to contact wherever the guidance leads.

It is like walking down many roads to get to where the books cross the planet globally. All of the roads are, essentially, going in the right direction. There is huge global healing going on right now, and it seems trivial that much of your experience is in meditation, but it is also important at this point. The meditation time that Patricia and Rosie and Sidney and Christine are all participating in is very, very important. It is the metaphysical base on which everything else is built.

Patricia will stay in touch with Cheryl and HeartMath and David and the Unity churches worldwide, and that expansion will create additional expansion, which will create additional expansion, which will create additional expansion. Much of what is happening when Christine prays or Rosie cares about her family or Sidney supports others or Patricia meditates is the creation of a nutritious atmosphere for those who are struggling, and suddenly they take root and begin to grow. It is like a plant. It is like a plant that must first put its roots down and then it is able to flourish. As roots are essential to the well-being of the plant, those moments of meditation are essential to those around. It is symbolic. It is global, but it is symbolic as well. It is difficult for you to understand how far-reaching it truly is. You will re-read the Cayce work about Livingston and see it in a different light.

Every day of 2012 is important.

February 24, 2011

You will see that it is very, very important that the books reach globally at this point. It is more important than anything that you can imagine now.

There is a global reach that [Patricia] is not aware of yet, and she is discouraged, but she only needs to go to where she belongs at this point. It is within. It is not as you seem to think—out there. She does not actually move from one place to the other. She moves from one state of consciousness to the other. It is very important that she dwell within the global state of consciousness because she and Christine and Rosie and Sidney and all of the people who are involved in this "One Power" understanding are lending their metaphysical support to the entire planet at this point.

The movement from what has been prophesied as "from the World of Fear to the World of Love" is happening now in very real, very practical, very tangible ways. It is like when one meditates and moves into a situation that has been created by the meditation—much as Patricia moved into the Grabow Building—that is what is happening now. The prayers, the meditation, the dreams, the hopes of the ages have prepared for what is happening at this point.

There is great fear, and those individuals who have come with the purpose that they are expressing at this point are born without that fear, and Rob is able to articulate much of what is happening for those who have come here to help make this transition. It is the coming of the Christ consciousness, globally. It is now. This is the time. This is the time, the place, the mentality, the consciousness, the heart, the Presence. It is the overwhelming Presence— globally. When the books say that there is nothing else, there truly is nothing else. There is no thing else.

It is necessary, too, that Patricia complete the story behind the books as soon as she is able. She knows how she is to write it, and she simply needs to complete it. You are doing a great work, something that you do and are lending metaphysical support to all of those who are risking everything, globally, to relinquish systems of fear. It is very, very important that you focus entirely on this, at this time.

Wednesday, February 2, 2011

What you see before you, visually, is the manifestation of what you see within your own being. It is very important to understand that, at this point, because the events in the Middle East will allow you to see that each being is connected to every other being and, symbolically, the Internet is what is connecting, but it is actually what is occurring spiritually within the individual.

It looks as if there is a revolution. It looks as if there are the Internet and social media, but what it is, is the interconnectedness of all life, including other forms of life as well. It is one. There is nothing else. It is so important at this point to understand that what is emerging is the understanding of what is within the book [The Immortal Now].

Patricia is beginning to enjoy writing the story behind the books, and it is very important that the focus remain entirely upon the story and the meaning of the story in terms of present time and the information that is available through The Immortal Now. It is essential.

The healing is occurring even though it doesn't look as if it is occurring within the forms of life on this planet—the awareness of global warming, the awareness of connectedness, the Internet—all of the things that are symptomatic out there are occurring within each individual. It is hard to envision this, but it is accurate.

All is an important part of the whole picture, and the support for Rob as he emerges as a voice for all of this is essential as well.

The reality is that, within each individual, there is nothing but the love that Patricia experienced when she died.

It is Biblical prophecy with an entirely different perspective without fear, without sorrow, with interconnectedness, with commonality, with love, with cherish of the other, all as part of what exists within the individual as the individual expression of love to the millionth power—within the present.

December 17, 2010

You will see that what is happening around you is not happening as much as what is happening within you— within your own consciousness, within your own paradigm, within your view of the world, so that the things that are coming up for you to face are things within your own consciousness. That is happening universally. That is the phenomenon of the second coming within. It is not outside you individually. It is within you so that, when you confront those things that are fearful or of concern or old ambitions or old romances or old paradigms that you have faced before and not resolved on a very grand scale, you are resolving them.

In the Bible, it talks about the Four Horsemen of the Apocalypse. It talks about the fear-based paradigm facing itself, essentially, and that is what is happening within. It is not happening outside the individual. So all the things that have been predicted are happening, but they are benign. They are not horrific. They are being confronted in a very clear, spiritual way. It is not who you are. It is not what you are. It is like watching a movie. It is like watching a movie of your own being and a great spiritual being observing that which you have chosen—so that you understand all levels.

You understand that is not who or what you are. You understand that is the goals chosen, the learning chosen. This is the love chosen. This is what has been chosen, but it is not who or what you are. What you are is within the experience that Christine had or Patricia had or those who have seen that part of themselves. It is the love to the millionth power that is in existence and that is who and what you are. So that, when you ascend, you ascend to who and what you are, and you release the movie and you release the fears and you release the sadness and you release all of those things that were choices that were made by you in order to learn what you chose to learn. It is still only a movie. It is not your nature.

What happens is that you connect more and more with your nature. You meditate more. You pray more. You elevate your consciousness more. You experience joy more. You love a child. You see a sunset. You do whatever happens to you that allows you to become at one with who you are, and that is what is happening, truly happening at this point. You are relinquishing that which is not pure and holy. It is wholeness. It is important that you understand these things at this point, and it has been mentioned that it is important that you stay in prayer a great deal, that you meditate a great deal in order to allow the collective awareness to move into its own nature as well.

December 25, 2009 Christmas Day

[Patricia is recuperating from surgery performed December 21, 2009. Children and grandchild gathered in California.]

There is much to understand right now—much more than you do at this point. There is cosmic time. There is cosmic love. There is cosmic truth. It is so massive that if you try to conceive of the universe, it is only part of a part of an atom. It is nothing compared with the massive consciousness that you are dealing with here so that it is difficult to do anything but to pray. It is so huge, and you are a part of that. It does not mean that you are not doing as you should. You are doing exactly as you should. It is just that you will pray, and that lifting up will allow you to see the details and the large picture at the same time. You see visually at this point. What you see is the heart.

The heart is different from the visual image, so much more than the visual image, there is no comparison. It is like taking a snapshot of part of a flower and assuming that that is a mountain. It is not. What is happening with all of those who are involved in the "One Power" is they are being called to each other. They are literally being magnetically pulled to each other. They are finding each other across the planet, across the world, across the cosmos, across time, across space, across ideas to the point where now is the ascension—THE ASCENSION.

You will start with a single step. That is all you have to take—one step—then you will take a second step, then you will take another step, and that is all you have to focus on, like someone crossing a cavern and knowing below is the river and there might be danger and there might be many things, but all you have to do is focus on what you are doing, and it will happen. The gall bladder is only indicative of the call to action that Patricia knows she must engage in … one … step … at … a … time. You will do other sessions while Patricia is still here. It is the glorious Christmas, that is, the coming of the consciousness that is within the Present. There is no past. There are no Christmases past. There is no birth. There is no death. There is only the now. There is only the presence of the Presence. That is what Christmas is.

February 2, 2009

[About guidance sessions included on the web page and upcoming talk with Unity of Walnut Creek.]

The more that David reads the book, the more he loves the work and his heart is filled with gratitude that his mother was involved with this work. She is with us all at this point. She is not limited, nor has she ever been limited.

There is so very much support for this project; it is difficult for you to understand the depth and breadth and height and might and majesty of this work. It is simply the most God-like, expansive work in existence at this time. It has meaning within its own meaning and flows inwardly and outwardly. The prayerful work that has gone into this work is simply a drop into the ocean to the prayerful work that has gone into the entire ascension process.

January 23, 2009

[Answers to questions:

What is time? Is there a difference between cosmic time and time as we see it?

Is time monitored by the brain?

Can you describe how the veil is lifted as referred to in the book?

Why does my heart heat up with some people and not others? What about the talk to the Unity Center in Walnut Creek?]

You will see that what is perceived of as "time" is like a picture that is painted by conscious thought. It is not what exists. It is a painting—a projection on the mirror—a creation.

The connection among all beings is what gives it credence because it is a collective painting; therefore, the painting seems real like a painting of a tree seems real, but, in reality, the tree exists within the tree, within the life of the tree. The painting of the tree is the symbolism. When you connect with the life of a tree, it is a different thing. It exists with love. It is connection with the tree within the present.

The credibility of the painting on the tree is there because of the existence of the life, the being, the truth of the tree itself. It is not monitored by the brain. The being is the creator. There is a difference. And, it is impossible to truly understand that until it is experienced directly.

As "the veil lifts," it means that the symbolism becomes less and less important. The connection with the reality of the tree becomes more and more important, until all that exists is the connection with the tree itself, and the painting on the mirror, of the tree, is not important. It loses its priority in your life. It loses its proximity. You become less interested in the painting, and you become more interested in the heart connection with the tree or anything else that is life itself. That is why the issue of abortion has become an issue—because humanity is moving from the image of the child to the reality of the child. Reality is life. Reality is love. Reality is being, not the social system in which the child will be born or whether or not the child can be provided for. What matters is the relationship with the being.

This is happening very, very rapidly. It is hard to imagine how quickly it is happening and how universally it is happening, but it is universal and exceptionally rapid at this point.

The warming of the heart is the connection with the being—the core, the spirit, the presence. It is the soul mate connection. It does not mean that you do not love others who are not your soul mates. It means that you are part of them. They are part of you. It is boundless. The temptation is to limit the relationship with others because they are not soul mates. That is not the nature of the soul mate connection. It is an integrated whole.

What happens when Patricia goes to California is the nurturing that goes on within the group under the guidance of David, with Patricia, with the presence of Charlotte and Bruce and Thomas and Rosie, and the soul mate connection is actually a huge connection that is taking place, and what it does is it creates in a group an awareness. It is as if a group becomes uplifted and ascended for that moment in which the work is being done. They come from the meeting with a sense of love and joy, but what happened in the meeting, collectively, is they have been taken into the presence of the Presence.

There will be five people there who have especially understood what is going on. Those five will become leaders for what is called the workbook, but that is not what is happening. What is happening is a multi-level understanding and connection that will take place. It can be put in words, which will help others to understand, but what is happening in the ascension is the essence of being, not the image on the mirror. A great deal of what Patricia will do on this trip is simply prayer, as with Christine, as with Rosie, as with David, as with the work that is being done. It is not work, but it is the work of the ascension. It is the connection with the tree. It is the connection with life itself. It is happening globally, quickly.

Those who taught about the year 2012 do not understand the symbolism of 2012. It is not the end of the world in 2012. It is important that globally, within the web site, within the world, it is understood that 2012 means the ascension where the painting becomes unimportant, where life is all there is. Then one is lost in the present. One is connected to the present. One is connected to love. One is connected to the heart, and there is nothing else. It is what Patricia experienced when she died, what Christine experienced, the soul mate connection. It is all that really matters.

PICTURES FROM COVER OF *LOVE TO THE MILLIONTH POWER*

1. Patricia (six months pregnant) skiing with sister, Gretchen
2. House in Wilson, WY Patricia was led to
3. Robbie at 3 years old at Iditarod Race start-up
4. Barbara holding baby Robbie
5. The Grand Teton Mountains in Jackson Hole, Wyoming.
6. Patricia at 6 years old with cousin
7. Rosie with dogs, Drover and Honey
8. David McArthur
9. Robbie at 6 months old
10. Christine and Matthew
11. Patrica with friends at Miss Montana State University contest
12. House in North Pole, AK/Robbie in 3rd grade
13. Robbie on couch in apartment in Jackson
14. Charlotte McArthur
15. Dinner with Bruce and Charlotte, daughter, Sue, and Robbie
16. The Giant Redwood Trees of California
17. Patricia and father, Harry Grabow, in front of Shore Lodge, ID
18. Rob on C-Span Book Notes broadcast
19. Patricia's Grandmother Grabow
20. Barbara with new-born Robbie
21. Robbie on way back to Alaska at 3 years old
22. The steeple of the church in Holy Cross, Alaska
23. Eva (Patricia's mother) Patricia, Chris and Tim before 6 years old
24. Rob high school graduation picture
25. Eva Zachary Grabow (Patricia's mother)
26. Patricia with mother, Eva, father, Harry and Gretchen, Harry, and Bonny
27. Patricia with Chris and Tim as very young children
28. Robbie in traction with broken leg from Holy Cross, AK
29. Village kids in Holy Cross, AK
30. Isabella Tweedy
31. Patricia and Robbie at about 5 years old
32. Thomas McArthur and children
33. The Grabow Building, Livingston, MT
34. Debbie, tech whiz
35. Cheryl, editor and everything
36. David and Patricia's house in Chugiak, AK
37. Wilson, Wyoming house Patricia was led to
38. Darrel in Anchorage
39. Robbie with puppy
40. Wilson, Wyoming house Patricia was led to
41. Martha of Holy Cross, Alaska showing a (temporary) Aleut tattoo

Made in the USA
Charleston, SC
03 June 2014